BUILDING
PROOFREADING
SKILLS

by Leland Graham and Isabelle McCoy

Incentive Publications, Inc.
Nashville, Tennessee

ACKNOWLEDGMENTS

The authors gratefully acknowledge the assistance
and suggestions of the following persons:

Virginia Brickman, Chris Higgins, Helen Jones, Martha
Lee, Frankie Long, Billie Mason, Jonathan McCoy,
Beverly Moody, Jennifer Moore, and Patricia Slaton.

Illustrated by Marta Drayton
Cover by Geoffrey Brittingham
Edited by Tama Montgomery and Anna Quinn

Table of Contents

Introduction

To the Teacher

Proofreading, in general usage, is the close examination of anything written before it is put into its final form for dissemination, including books, magazines, newspapers, newsletters, correspondence, and pamphlets.

The purpose of **Building Proofreading Skills** is to assist your students in learning and using basic proofreading techniques. It is the authors' intention to provide a selection of creative, even enjoyable, activities to encourage students to develop these essential, lifelong writing skills.

Proofreading skills are employed from the time the first grader writes that first three-letter spelling word on a test until well beyond the doctoral student's multiple revisions of a dissertation. It is never too early to begin teaching the skills and habits of good proofreading.

For the sake of organization, the opening chapters of this book have been divided into the usual segments: spelling, capitalization, punctuation, and grammar. The concluding chapters contain longer selections for proofreading as well as writing prompts for students to create their own works to be proofread. This book also contains a number of creative ideas for moving the task of proofreading from the teacher to the students.

On page five is a list of commonly used proofreading and editing symbols. While the authors realize that proofreading symbols vary from book to book, these symbols are among the most commonly used. Your students will need to become familiar with these symbols before attempting to complete the exercises in this book. The authors highly recommend that each student receive a permanent copy of the proofreading symbols.

The answer key reflects the proofreading system explained on page five; therefore, if your students are familiar with a different system, answers may vary. Furthermore, there are often several ways to correctly punctuate, and the answer key does not reflect all of these options.

Proofreading and Editing Symbols

Proofreading symbols are used to identify mistakes and to state the needed correction. Listed below are the most common proofreading symbols, along with explanation and examples of each.

Symbol	Explanation of the Symbol	Example
¶	Begin a new paragraph	¶He explained the rules of
≡	Capitalize a lowercase letter	Henderson middle School
/	Use a lowercase letter	great skiing trips in the Winter
∧ or ∨	Insert a missing word, letter, or punctuation mark	My friend Joe has a new green car.
⌒	Close up space	Some body will help you soon.
ℯ	Delete and close up	taught my sister etiqquette
ℯ	Delete a word, letter, or punctuation mark	Joy gave two too many reasons.
SP	Spell out	SP the 30 thirty inches of fabric
∽	Change the order of letters or words	In the ursh of leaving, he forgot
tr	Move the circled words to the place marked by the arrow (write *tr* in the margin.)	The young boys threw for the cows over the fence some hay tr
⊙	Add a period	The problem was easily solved⊙
⋏	Add a comma	Well, I'll give it a chance.
#	Add a space	Toni used#the money to start
:/	Add a colon	The letter read: "Dear Mr. Yen"
;/	Add a semicolon	I'll help you now; it's not hard.
⌃	Add a hyphen	lives on Twenty-third Street
∨	Add an apostrophe	Jonathan's new computer
⁀ ⁀	Insert quotation marks	Sally said, Good morning.
stet	The **stet** in the margin means "stay;" let marked text stay as written. Place three dots under original text.	stet My father was rather angry at . . .

©1999 by Incentive Publications, Inc.
Nashville, TN.

Chapter 1

Building Proofreading Skills in Spelling

Spelling mistakes can prevent others from seeing your great ideas in print. This chapter will help you learn to avoid common spelling errors through a variety of carefully selected activities. Many spelling mistakes come from careless haste. Whenever you write, proofread your paper not only for difficult words, but also for simple, ordinary words that you may have misspelled through carelessness.

How to Improve Your Spelling of Particular Words:
1. Find out what your personal spelling demons are and conquer them.
2. Keep a good dictionary nearby to use whenever in doubt.
3. Pronounce words correctly; this will help you write them correctly.
4. Get into the habit of taking a good look at new or difficult words.
5. Develop your own memory device (called a **mnemonic**) for difficult words.

PRETEST: Each item below gives four possible spellings of a word. Read the words, and circle the letter of the correct spelling.

Sample:

a. apoligize (b.) apologize c. eplogize d. epoligize

1. a. formela   b. fourmula   c. formula   d. foremulla

2. a. concession   b. concesion   c. consetion   d. consession

3. a. gratfull   b. grateful   c. greatful   d. gradeful

4. a. annoience   b. annoiance   c. anoyence   d. annoyance

5. a. hastily   b. hastilie   c. hastely   d. hastyly

6. a. triplacate   b. tripleacate c. triplicate   d. triplicte

7. a. justefid   b. justified   c. justifyed   d. justifeyed

8. a. stabillaty   b. stabbility   c. stabilaty   d. stability

Name _____

©1999 by Incentive Publications, Inc.
Nashville, TN.

Building Proofreading Skills in Spelling

ie and ei Spelling Errors

Rule 1: Write *ie* when the sound is *long e (grief, believe, relief)*, except after *c (deceive, receive, conceive)*. **Exceptions:** *neither, leisure, seize*

Rule 2: Write *ei* when the sound is not *long e*, especially when the sound is *long a (sleigh, foreign, freight)*. **Exceptions:** *friend, mischief, soldier*

ACTIVITY: Proofread the following paragraph. Add either *ie* or *ei* to complete the words.

Sample:

The for**ei**gn sold**ie**r accidentally dropped his sh**ie**ld in the f**ie**ld.

Recently our n____ghborhood held its annual picnic in the baseball f____ld near the ch____f of police's house. We ate lots of food— w____ners, corn on the cob, and p____ces of cake. Some of the people started playing w____rd games, combining softball and soccer. While we were playing ball, the misch____vous children said they saw a th____f race through the picnic area and rel____ve us of all the sandwiches. My n____ce did not bel____ve them, so she began to give the children gr____f. One of her fr____nds said that he saw the real th____ves.

Suddenly, the smiling children returned the sandwiches, and we enjoyed the rest of our l____sure time. At the end of the afternoon, our grandfather presented special ach____vement awards to all except the "misch____vous" children.

Name _____

Building Proofreading Skills in Spelling

-able and -ible Spelling Errors

Because the *-able* and *-ible* endings usually sound the same, sound is not a good clue to use when deciding which spelling to use. A good general rule to remember is that *-able* occurs more often as a suffix than *-ible*.

Rule 1: If the word ends in a consonant followed by an *e*, the *e* is dropped before adding *-ible* or *-able*. **Exceptions:** words ending in *ce* or *ge*, such as *noticeable* and *knowledgeable.*

Rule 2: If a word ends in *y*, add the suffix *-able*, not *-ible*. The *y* will change to *i* as in *reliable,* or it will drop as in *charitable.*

ACTIVITY: Each item below lists four possible spellings of a word. Read the words, and circle the letter of the correct spelling.

Sample:

a. charartible	(b.) charitable	c. charatable	d. charitible

1. a. iratible	b. irritable	c. iritable	d. irratable
2. a. relieable	b. relible	c. relyable	d. reliable
3. a. reducible	b. reducable	c. reduceable	d. reduceible
4. a. legable	b. leggible	c. legible	d. leggable
5. a. comvertable	b. convirtible	c. convertable	d. convertible
6. a. misrible	b. miserable	c. misrable	d. misarible
7. a. respectable	b. respectible	c. respecable	d. respecible
8. a. incredable	b. increable	c. incredible	d. increible
9. a. imaginible	b. imagenable	c. imaginable	d. immaginable
10. a. indisputable	b. indesputible	c. innisputable	d. indisputible

Name _____

©1999 by Incentive Publications, Inc.
Nashville, TN.

Building Proofreading Skills in Spelling

-ant, -ent, -ance, and -ence Spelling Errors

In words with the *-ant, -ent, -ance,* or *-ence* endings, sound is not a very good clue to the spelling of the ending. There is, however, a good way to remember whether a word is spelled with *-ant* or *-ent*, or whether it is spelled with *-ance* or *-ence.* Look at the following word pairs:

assist<u>ant</u>—assist<u>ance</u>   intellig<u>ent</u>—intellig<u>ence</u>

The words in each pair are related in meaning and in spelling. So, if you are uncertain about whether the spelling of an ending is *-ant* or *-ent*, or *-ance* or *-ence*, think of the related word.

ACTIVITY: Proofread the following paragraph, using *-ant, -ent, -ance,* or *-ence* to complete the words. Write the correct letters in each blank.

Sample:

The opening number in the award-winning musical was quite magnific**ent.**

When our test scores were returned last week, Mr. Thomas announced that we had made signific_____ improvement. He was pleased with our overall, brilli_____ scores. For the first time ever, Mr. Thomas filled our class with unbelievable confid_____. He also attributed part of the results to our outstanding attend_____ record.

Louise remarked, "Mr. Thomas, we all feel that your pati_____ has contributed a great deal to our ability to learn this year."

Another student stated gleefully, "Without your assist_____ in algebra, we would not feel as confid_____."

"Students," Mr. Thomas replied, "your intellig_____ has been there all along. I'm just so glad that I could help all of you realize your true, magnific_____ ability."

BONUS:

Write a few sentences or a short paragraph using words ending with *-ant, -ent, -ance,* and *-ence.* Spell some of the words correctly and some incorrectly. Then, exchange papers with a classmate to proofread.

Name _____

©1999 by Incentive Publications, Inc.
Nashville, TN.

Building Proofreading Skills in Spelling

-ary, -ery, and -ory Spelling Errors

Sometimes the sound of the ending is a good clue to its spelling, as in dormit*ory* and ordin*ary.* In many words, however, the vowel sounds are unaccented, and thus the sound is not a good clue to its spelling, as in batt*ery* and summ*ary.* **Hint:** Most of the time adjectives use the -ary ending, as in revolution*ary,* and nouns use the -ery ending, as in scen*ery.*

An Unusual Tour

Calinda and her sister Frieda arrived at the cemet_____ at 2 P.M. The tour of the city would begin there. The scen_____ was beautiful, although the tempor_____ shelter that had been erected at the site was very ordin_____.

Calinda wondered what kind of sal_____ the tour guides earn. Their tour guide seemed to have an extraordin_____ amount of knowledge about the hist_____ of the city. The guide began telling Frieda and Calinda about the myst_____ concerning one of the graves.

Apparently during the time of the Revolution_____ War, a man was accused of creating a forg_____ of a document. The man was believed to have been caught, killed, and buried in the cemet_____. However, when the grave was excavated much later, no body was found in the coffin.

After listening to the mysterious tale, the two sisters then toured the laborat_____ of a well-known scientist. Later, they visited a building that was used as a dormit_____ for a private school. The girls thoroughly enjoyed their visit. They vowed to return even as they passed the bound_____ of the old city and set out toward home.

Name _____

Building Proofreading Skills in Spelling

Spelling Homonyms Correctly

Below is a list of commonly used **homonyms** (words that sound the same, but have different spellings and meanings) of which proofreaders need to be aware.

their	**to**	**rain**
there	**too**	**reign**
they're	**two**	**rein**
coarse	**threw**	**pear**
course	**through**	**pair**
stationary	**capital**	**who's**
stationery	**capitol**	**whose**
principal	**your**	
principle	**you're**	

ACTIVITY: Proofread the sentences below. Correct the misused homonyms, using the proofreading symbols, (see page 5) to insert or delete letters as needed.
Hint: When choosing a homonym, always think about what the word *means* in the sentence.

Sample:

Who's reference books are these on the table in the library?

1. The principle corrected the students in the hallway by repeating one of the golden principals.

2. Will you please pass the pear of gloves lying near the jar of pairs on the table.

3. Jill wrote her letter on the new lavender stationary since she had to remain stationery in her room for the afternoon.

4. To many children are going two several events during the too days of the festival.

5. Their are often too many students going to they're lockers when there supposed to be in there classes.

6. Remember to use a capitol letter when spelling Washington, D.C., our nation's capitol.

7. For you're science test, your required to learn the parts of a flower.

Name _____

©1999 by Incentive Publications, Inc.
Nashville, TN.

Building Proofreading Skills in Spelling

Spelling

ACTIVITY: Each item below gives three possible spellings of a word. Read the words, and circle the correct spelling.

Sample:

trater	triater	(traitor)
1. athelete	athalete	athlete
2. library	libeary	libary
3. February	Febuary	Febrary
4. govenor	govener	governor
5. angal	angle	angol
6. arthur	author	althur
7. sincerely	sinserely	sincerly
8. rythm	rhythm	rhithm
9. unusual	unusal	unusuall
10. musel	mussul	muscle
11. tomatos	tomatoess	tomatoes
12. photoe	foto	photo
13. separate	seperate	sepparate
14. pressence	presence	prescence
15. omited	omitted	ommitted
16. aukward	awkword	awkward

BONUS:

Make a list of ten words that you misspell often, spelling them incorrectly. Then give the list to a classmate to proofread and correct.

Name _____

©1999 by Incentive Publications, Inc.
Nashville, TN.

Building Proofreading Skills in Spelling

Spelling

ACTIVITY: Proofread the following phrases. In most of the phrases, there will be one misspelled word. Underline the misspelled word and, in the blank provided, write the word correctly. If there are no misspelled words, write **none** in the blank.

Sample

at the new Olympic Stadium in Atlanta _____ *none* _____

1. must tell people of your true fellings _____

2. think carefully about your own writting _____

3. the unusual statement of porpose _____

4. refusse to be closely involved _____

5. to discover her own natural ability _____

6. enables the large, beautiful bird to fly _____

7. his unbiased political opinon of the candidate _____

8. due north of metropolitin Chicago _____

9. to talk Carlos out of atending the football game _____

10. the old ferosious lion in the zoo _____

11. destined to win the state championship title _____

12. seemed totally asttonished about the murder _____

13. intervue the anxious applicant at the office _____

14. tall, muscular, intense marshell at the jail _____

15. caught a quick glimse of the movie star _____

Name _____

©1999 by Incentive Publications, Inc.
Nashville, TN.

Building Proofreading Skills in Spelling

Spelling

ACTIVITY: Proofread each sentence carefully and circle the misspelled words. Then write the correct spelling on the blanks provided. You may not need all of the blanks.

Sample:

At the (delicatesen) they served delicious ham sandwiches.   *delicatessen*

1. The Atlanta Braves' uniforms have a red
   tomahwak on the front.

   _____

   _____

2. On this particuler evening, we went to the
   nearby restaurant to eat steak and potatoes.

   _____

   _____

3. The old woman beleived that the pathetic
   begger was truly in desperate need.

   _____

   _____

4. The county ambulence raced quickly to the
   tragic scene of the traffic accidant.

   _____

   _____

5. One rhinoceros was slautered for his valuable horn.

   _____

6. When the two old friends met, they sat and
   began to reminise about their childhood.

   _____

   _____

7. The magnifisence of the sunset was indescribable.

   _____

8. The temperature in the Artic was extremely
   friggid all year long.

   _____

   _____

9. I wonder if that animal I saw in the woods was a
   racoon or an opossum.

   _____

   _____

10. Is a canteloup considered a vegatable or a fruit?

    _____

    _____

11. The clever theives were thorogh when they robbed
    the house.

    _____

    _____

12. Ashley and her freind finaly decided to go to the movies.

    _____

    _____

Name _____

Building Proofreading Skills in Spelling

Spelling

ACTIVITY: Proofread the following paragraphs for spelling errors. Circle the misspelled words and then, on the line provided, write the correct spelling of each word.

Sample:

The (wonerful) employees at Della's Gift Shop were
treated to a dinner party (honering) all employees who
had served over five years.

wonderful

honoring

Snakes

Snakes are in the repitile family and are closely related to _____

lizards. They are covered with numberous small scales, which are _____

overlapping. They have moveable eyelids and external ear _____

openings. They use their toungues to smell. The smallest snake is _____

8–12 inches long and the largest meausures about 8 feet. _____

Snakes are carniveres, which means they are meat-eaters. _____

They find their pray by smell and sight, but they don't see well. _____

They eat their prey whole. Some snakes kill by constrition, some by _____

prompt swalowing, and others kill by poisoning. Their jaws aren't _____

atachhed and this helps them swallow their food. Their teeth also _____

aid them in eatting. Many snakes eat rats and mice, and it may _____

take 4–6 days to digest a meal. Some snakes are beleived _____

to be able to go two years without food.

From: *Effective Language Arts Techniques for Middle Grades,* by
Brenda Opie and Douglas McAvinn, Incentive Publications,
Nashville, Tennessee, 1995.

Building Proofreading Skills in Spelling

Spelling

ACTIVITY: Here's a real challenge in proofreading for spelling errors! First, look at the list of words below and circle the correct spelling of each word. Next, read the sentences and, in the blank provided, write the correct spelling of the word that best completes each sentence.

proceed	OR	prosede
recieved	OR	received
circuit	OR	sircuit
exceed	OR	exsede
voloenteered	OR	volunteered
prospector	OR	prospecter
sucede	OR	succeed
miserible	OR	miserable
patiance	OR	patience
divisible	OR	divisable
excelerate	OR	(accelerate)

Sample:

The car began to ___**accelerate**___ rapidly down the road.

1. The electric _____ was overloaded and caused a fire.

2. How will the meeting _____ without our chairperson?

3. Munga wanted to _____ Maria as Henderson student council president.

4. The police officer warned us not to _____ the speed limit in her town.

5. Please demonstrate your _____ while waiting for your appointment.

6. Is the number 56 _____ by 8 or 6?

7. Natasha was certainly _____ after her appendectomy.

8. Umar, our exchange student from Saudi Arabia, _____ to help us.

9. The _____ went into the Rockies and struck gold immediately.

10. When I attended the Garth Brooks concert, he _____ a standing ovation.

Name _____

Building Proofreading Skills in Spelling

Spelling

ACTIVITY: Proofread the following paragraphs for spelling errors. Circle all the misspelled words. Then, write the correct spelling of each misspelled word on the line provided.

Sample:

(Antartica) the coolest place on earth, is the fifth largest   *__Antarctica__*

continent. This ice-covered area (completly) encircles the   *__completely__*

South Pole.

VACATION AT MULBERRY POND
(JOURNAL: JUNE 20, 19__)

Colors of mostly orange and yellow began to drifft in the sky as   _____

a welcomming sunrise fell upon Mulberry in the warm morning that I   _____

arrived. Rays of gold danced on the pond, beckkening me to the   _____

water to soothe the summer heat. Haridly waiting for the car to come   _____

to a standstill, I imediattely dashed for the pond, with renewed   _____

memories of last summer and what lay in store for me

this summer.

Retreeting to this secluded log cabin out in the middle of the   _____

forest has been our family tradtion for years. The pond reaches out   _____

into the pine trees, giving beauty to the surounding, wilderness.   _____

Accustomed to friendly human life, animals rome the area with the   _____

same kind of contenment that the pond seems to reflect. And the   _____

lush green grass around the pond wilingly supports all kinds of   _____

ladybugs and butterflies.

From: *Preparing Students to Raise Achievement Scores* [Grades 5–6], by Leland Graham and Darriel Ledbetter, Incentive Publications, Inc., Nashville, Tennessee, 1996.

Name _____

Chapter 2

Building Proofreading Skills in Capitalization

Because it is important to learn how to communicate with written language, proper capitalization is essential. The purpose of this chapter is to develop and improve your capitalization skills in proofreading. Remember, proper nouns, pronouns, and proper adjectives are capitalized, and the first word in every sentence is capitalized. Working through these carefully selected exercises will improve your writing skills as well as your capitalization and proofreading skills.

PRETEST: Proofread each sentence carefully. Use the proofreading symbol for capitalization (see page 5), to correct each word that should be capitalized.

Sample:

We enjoyed french bread with our meal.

1. Were you born in december?

2. I met prince Charles in london.

3. Sue enjoyed reading *little women.*

4. it happened the last day of january.

5. what is the population of china now?

6. Tom said, "i need a new skateboard."

7. halloween, my favorite holiday, is in october.

8. Our class visited rabbi rosenbaum.

9. my favorite book is *sounder.*

10. carrie's mother bought a new mustang.

11. mail the letter to mayor campbell.

12. Our school has many spanish students.

13. Our family went to florida for vacation.

14. My brother attends columbia university.

15. We crossed the golden gate bridge.

16. My sister joined the girl scouts.

17. please finish your reports by thursday.

18. We thought uncle walter had arrived.

Name _____

©1999 by Incentive Publications, Inc.
Nashville, TN.

Building Proofreading Skills in Capitalization

Capitalization

ACTIVITY: Read the following list of words. In each line there is one word that does not require a capital letter. On the blank provided, write the word that does not require any capitalization.

> **Rule 1:** Capitalize proper nouns and proper adjectives *(July, Buddhist)*.
>
> **Rule 2:** Capitalize geographical names *(Haiti, Atlantic Ocean)*.
>
> **Rule 3:** Capitalize a person's title only if followed by their name *(doctor, Doctor Smith)*.
>
> **Rule 4:** Capitalize the pronoun *I*.

Sample:

Melinda	February	Senator	Bolivia	___*senator*___

1.	Joseph	Laos	Doctor	England	_____
2.	France	Mister	Melinda	Congress	_____
3.	President	Elizabeth	Ed	Donald	_____
4.	Dallas	Aunt	America	Halloween	_____
5.	Mother	Sunday	Ohio	Ontario	_____
6.	Swedish	Europe	Queen	Georgia	_____
7.	I'm	Isn't	I'd	I'll	_____
8.	Billy	Spanish	Asia	Actor	_____
9.	Paris	Avenue	Peru	California	_____
10.	Burma	Martha	Spain	Island	_____
11.	Liberty	Russian	Jonathan	June	_____
12.	Harriett	Roger	Desert	Mississippi	_____
13.	Patricia	City	Bianca	Patrick	_____
14.	August	Thursday	Caesar	Street	_____
15.	Easter	Africa	Winter	Beverly	_____

Name _____

©1999 by Incentive Publications, Inc.
Nashville, TN.

Building Proofreading Skills in Capitalization

Capitalization

ACTIVITY: Using all of the previuosly stated rules of capitalization, proofread the following phrases for errors. Use the proofreading symbols for capitalization (see page 5) to mark the word(s) that should be capitalized. Hint: Some phrases do not contain any errors in capitalization. If there are no mistakes in the phrase, write **none** to the left of the phrase.

Sample:

the postcard I sent to jim

1. one of our police officers

2. president Wilson of the United States

3. just the other day my dad and bob

4. aunt rose, one of my favorite aunts,

5. here at Westlake mall we always

6. billy, my brother's nickname,

7. to his favorite doctor, doctor cook,

8. the number of the new house on oak street

9. into the cold water of the lake

10. always wanted to live as a southeasterner

11. to lake superior after their wedding

12. roads like Beverly Hills' rodeo drive

13. a 1965 ford mustang in perfect condition

14. driving to the southeast side of the city

15. at sutton middle school in Atlanta, Georgia

BONUS:

Write a short paragraph about one of your heroes. Include several errors in capitalization. Exchange papers with one of your classmates to proofread.

Name _____

Building Proofreading Skills in Capitalization

Capitalization

ACTIVITY: Using all of the rules of capitalization, proofread the following sentences for errors. Use the proofreading symbols for capitalization (see page 5) to mark the word(s) that should be capitalized and those that should be lowercase.

Sample:

The new Student, Jason Richards, is originally from toledo, ohio.

1. When we were in Wyoming last Summer, We visited yellowstone national Park.

2. when we last saw Sheri, she was driving West on McDonough street.

3. The tara theater is located near the Hotel on Cheshire Bridge road.

4. one of the most breathtaking bridges in the world is the golden gate bridge.

5. My Grandmother visited the smoky mountains where thousands of cherokee Indians live.

6. In just a few minutes, the president of the United States will address congress.

7. Norway, Sweden, denmark, and Finland make up the scandinavian Countries.

8. While my Father was waiting to interview the Mayor, he read the *miami Herald.*

9. When school begins, I will be taking English, spanish, world History, and science.

10. Alex Haley, the author of *roots,* traced the History of his own family.

11. Many of the Cereal Companies have lowered their prices.

12. one of my favorite television shows is *friends,* which airs every thursday Night.

13. During the spring holidays, we visited Disneyworld and toured universal studios.

14. The reverend William McKoy introduced the renowned speaker, dr. wai phing choo.

15. Please mail your reply to 4536 North Druid hills road, atlanta, GA 30329.

16. Edgar has been a Member of the young men's Christian Association for 12 years.

17. let's ask bishop Wendell to give the commencement address.

18. One of my favorite books from last year's readings was *animal farm.*

19. If you want to get to Shady Valley Park, go North on Lenox road.

Name

©1999 by Incentive Publications, Inc.
Nashville, TN.

Building Proofreading Skills in Capitalization

Capitalization

ACTIVITY: Proofread the following phrases. Use the proofreading symbol for lowercase (see page 5) to mark the word(s) that should NOT be capitalized. *Hint:* Some phrases do not contain any mistakes in capitalization.

> **Rule 1:** Capitalize the first word in a sentence, not in a phrase.
> **Rule 2:** Capitalize the main words in the name of an important document.
> **Rule 3:** Capitalize the names of ships, planets, monuments, awards, and any particular places, parks, things, or historical events.
> **Rule 4:** Capitalize the names of nationalities, races, and religions.
> **Rule 5:** Do not capitalize the names of school subjects, except languages and course names followed by a number.

Sample:

the favorite *P*oet of all time

1. every year my Family travels through

2. chose a seat on the East side

3. while writing the Declaration of Independence

4. climbed the Highest Mountain in the world

5. Elizabeth, the Queen of England

6. days when my Brother and I spend time together

7. ate Swedish Pancakes for breakfast

8. the Chinese Manager of Yung's new company

9. the last name of the Princess of Monaco

10. my favorite part of the Country

11. watched the Pilot land the Plane on the runway

12. took a tour of the Museum

13. the Fourth Thursday in November

14. in the Beautiful Spring weather

15. an African-American woman we studied in History

16. on the Ship the *S.S. Queen Elizabeth*

Name _____

©1999 by Incentive Publications, Inc.
Nashville, TN.

Building Proofreading Skills in Capitalization

Capitalization

ACTIVITY: Proofread the following sentences for errors in capitalization. Using the proofreading symbols for lowercase and capitalization (see page 5), mark those word(s) that should be capitalized and those that should NOT be capitalized.

Rule 1: The first word of a sentence that is a direct quotation is capitalized even if the quotation begins within another sentence *(Marcie shouted, "She did it!")*

Rule 2: Capitalize the first word and all important words in titles of magazines, books, newspapers, poems, stories, movies, and works of art *(Roots)*.

Rule 3: Capitalize names of organizations, business firms, institutions, and government bodies *(Future Teachers of America)*.

Sample:

my aunt Sandy from salt lake City is a good Mother to all of her children.

1. "oh no," said mother, " i never told john that he could go to the concert."

2. How does the Doctor feel about the Treatment of his Cancer?

3. Poonam and her Sister have gone to the Store to buy some vegetables and fruit.

4. On Jekyll Island, off the coast of georgia, there is a 4-h facility.

5. King Ferdinand and his Queen did not want to give the Explorer any money.

6. How did the governor of california manage to accomplish all of his Goals?

7. in the state of south dakota, you will find mount rushmore.

8. The Book, *The Red pony,* by John Steinbeck is set during the Great depression.

9. roberto likes to watch the latin american dancers in their beautiful costumes.

10. Inga enjoys reading the national geographic magazine.

11. *The pet detective,* starring Jim Carey, is perhaps my favorite Movie.

12. Gandhi spoke spanish, german, and french as well as his native language, hindi.

13. "Where The Sidewalk Ends" by shel silverstein is one of my favorite Poems.

14. Did you know that kwanzaa is celebrated in december by many african-Americans?

15. In mexico my friends celebrate cinco de mayo in the Spring.

Name _____

©1999 by Incentive Publications, Inc.
Nashville, TN.

Building Proofreading Skills in Capitalization

Capitalization

ACTIVITY: Using all of the previously stated rules of capitalization, proofread the following phrases for errors. Use the proofreading symbols for lowercase and capitalization (see page 5) to mark the word(s) that should be capitalized as well as those that should NOT be capitalized.

Sample:

the Part of niagara falls in the United States

1. to get to my house from oakland city Schools

2. an odd Area of the atlantic ocean

3. a winding River bordering illinois and iowa

4. the Battlefield at Gettysburg, pennsylvania

5. the atacama desert in the South American Country of chile

6. six blocks South of North Druid Hills road

7. a well-known eastern University in Massachusetts

8. the biggest Football Game of the year

9. in 1492 christopher columbus and his Crew

10. in the Movie, *the Shawshank redemption*

11. My Short Story, "The King Of The court"

12. in the *New York Times* Article on sunday

13. athens, the Home of the University Of georgia

14. north of the caribbean Island of puerto rico

15. is celebrated with Parades in New York city

16. during the great depression of the 1930s

17. boarded the amtrak train in Carlsbad, New mexico

18. To open our Textbooks to Chapter 10 Today

Name

Building Proofreading Skills in Capitalization

Capitalization

ACTIVITY: From the following students' original paragraphs, correct any errors in capitalization by using the proofreading symbols (see page 5).

My Basketball Hero
by Bob Wechsler

I simply love the game of Basketball, and I chose Anfernee "penny" Hardaway as my Basketball Hero. He plays for the orlando Magic. The reasons i chose him are his Attitude and focus on his Goals. Whether It is on or Off the Basketball Court, "penny" stays focused. I would like to be as focused on my Personal goals and be as successful as Hardaway.

Martin Luther King, Jr., My Hero
by Alexandra Lentz

i consider dr. Martin Luther King, jr., to be a Hero because he was determined and dedicated to his work. dr. King was a good leader and wanted to help other people. He fought for the Freedom of African-americans, and now his Dream has come true. He was so determined that people finally changed the Laws. He also gave people Ideas to think about.

My Mother, My Hero
by Kemit Finch

Mrs. ellen Finch, my Mother, is also my hero. Her ability to understand me is her Strength. Responsibility is a big part of her Life. No matter what the circumstances, She always gets the job done. i praise her for her reminders. I probably would have failed at least one class (english) if she had not helped me with my homework. She is strict, never letting Anyone get the best of her, but she always has room for fun.

Name _____

©1999 by Incentive Publications, Inc.
Nashville, TN.

Building Proofreading Skills in Capitalization

Capitalization

ACTIVITY: Use the proofreading symbols (see page 5) to correct the errors in capitalization from Brandon Barnett's "Space Exploration" paper.

Space Exploration
by Brandon Barnett

The u.s. and many other Countries plan to start Colonizing Space. This project will be an International effort. Plans for an international Space Station are in the making. this project will be used to help the World control its population problem.

n.a.s.a. has already made plans to start building an International Space Station by the year 2000. The parts will be ferried up by the Space Shuttle over a period of several missions. Millions of Dollars will be spent for the Astronauts to accomplish this job.

If this Project is a success, people will start moving to self-contained Colonies. The countries of england, france, and the united states have already started pouring Dollars into this project.

colonizing Planets will give People the chance to explore new Frontiers. At one time this was only a dream, but in the future it will become a Reality.

BONUS:
Write a paragraph about a historic place that you have visited or would like to visit. Include errors in capitalization. Give the unedited paragraph to a classmate to proofread.

Name _____

Building Proofreading Skills in Capitalization
Cumulative Review
Spelling and Capitalization

ACTIVITY: Use the proofreading symbols (see page 5) to correct the errors in spelling and capitalization from Rachel Gottschalk's paper "The Scariest Night of My Life."

The Scariest Night of My Life
by Rachel Gottschalk

October 31, 1995, i was going Trick-or-Treatin with some of my freinds. I put on my costum and found my bag, just like any other hallowen night. Little did i know this would be the Scareist Night of My life (so far)!

we went the usuall route (around my nieghborhood), down Henderson mill road. When we were finisshed, it was only 8:00 P.M. My friends and i decided to try a new path. We went thorough glen rose street. By the time we were finisshed, our bags were full, and We were geting bored.

then one of my friends said, "you know that old Henderson cemetary near here? let's go there."

We all looked at each other, and Everyone agrreed we should go. I was a little scarred, but I couldn't chicken out now.

The Cemetary was so old that the stones had erroded and some of the graves had caved in. The lights were on in the nearby houses, so it was not too scarry. We were walking queitly through, when I sliped into one of the old Graves! (it may not seem scarry to you, but it scared me to death.)

my friends, who did not know what had hapened, screamed and ran. a few seconds later (it seemed like years), they realised i wasn't there and went back. My friends found me and helped me out of the Grave. You would not beleive how horiffied and disgusted i felt.

Later we went back to my house and "Pigged out" on all the candy. Our Adventur was somewhat scarry, but I would defanitily do it again.

Name _____

©1999 by Incentive Publications, Inc.
Nashville, TN.

Chapter 3

Building Proofreading Skills in Punctuation

Books and other pieces of writing would be difficult, if not impossible, to read if it were not for punctuation. Punctuation marks are similar to traffic signs. They warn the reader when to *slow down* (comma), when to *stop* (period, question mark, or exclamation mark), and when to be on the *lookout for something interesting or dangerous ahead* (quotation marks, underlining, hyphen, apostrophe, colon, semicolon, or parentheses).

The purpose of this chapter is to develop and improve your punctuation skills in proofreading. Working successfully through the following proofreading exercises will help you improve your punctuation skills.

PRETEST: Proofread the following sentences for end punctuation marks (**period, question mark,** and **exclamation mark**). Using the proofreading symbols (see page 5), add the appropriate punctuation mark to each sentence.

Sample:

Where is the beautiful vase that Aunt Martha gave me ?

1. Sing the song with me so that we can practice for the performance

2. When did the robin build that nest in the oak tree

3. That sunset is incredibly exquisite and inspiring

4. Tell Karina to call her house and speak to her mom

5. Why have you been talking on the phone for two hours

6. Seventh graders are such an awesome group of young people

7. Did you really enjoy your trip to Oregon

8. Sit down and begin taking notes on Chapter 14

9. Wow What an exciting football game

10. This lunch is one of the best we have had this year

Name _____

©1999 by Incentive Publications, Inc.
Nashville, TN.

Building Proofreading Skills in Punctuation

Period, Question Mark, and Comma

ACTIVITY: Proofread the following exercises for errors in punctuation (**period, question mark, and comma**). Using the proofreading symbols (see page 5), add the correct punctuation.

> **Rule 1:** Use a comma after the salutation of a friendly letter and after the closing of any letter (Dear Mary Lou,).
>
> **Rule 2:** Use a comma to separate items in dates and addresses (May 3, 1996).
>
> **Rule 3:** Appositives and appositive phrases are usually set off by commas (Harriett, my best friend,).
>
> **Rule 4:** An abbreviation is followed by a period (Aug.).
>
> **Rule 5:** Use a comma to separate city and state (Bangor, Maine).

Samples:

John F⊙Kennedy   Dr⊙A⊙Phillip Jones   Feb 15⊙1983↗

1. Cofer Bros Lumber Co is hiring workers until Sept 1 for their lumber yard

2. The private plane was landing at Charlie B Thomas Airfield during the storm

3. The minivan was traveling at only 55 mph on the Douglas P McDonald Freeway

4. My son Richard was born on Sept 25 1987 in Oklahoma City Oklahoma

5. Our family visited Springfield Illinois where President Lincoln practiced law

6. Did you receive your B A degree from Northwestern University

7.

July 10 1997

Dear Martha

We are pleased to invite you to Alicia's birthday party on Friday July 21 at 3 P M at Joe's Pizza Parlor on Memorial Drive

Sincerely

Name _____

©1999 by Incentive Publications, Inc.
Nashville, TN.

Building Proofreading Skills in Punctuation

Comma

ACTIVITY: Proofread the following sentences for errors in comma usage. Using the correct proofreading symbol (see page 5), add commas where necessary.

> **Rule 1:** Use commas to separate words in a series (eggs, milk, and cheese).
>
> **Rule 2:** Use a comma before *and, but, or, nor, for,* and *yet* when they join independent clauses. (Jim really likes golf, **but** he doesn't like tennis.)
>
> **Rule 3:** Parenthetical expressions are set off by commas. (**To be honest,** I thought the book was well written.)
>
> **Rule 4:** Use commas to set off introductory phrases and clauses. (**Since we have had no rain,** we have watered our lawn every day.)
>
> **Rule 5:** Use a comma to set off words used in direct address. (**Mr. Johnson,** come to the office immediately.)

Sample:

These bats balls and gloves need to go into the duffel bag.

1. The new girl on the block liked sailing but she did not like biking.

2. Maurice sang danced and played the harmonica for the talent show.

3. Our team if you can believe it won the championship last year.

4. During the Civil War life was very chaotic near the battlefields.

5. Tell me Louise if you can work for me on Thursday evening.

6. Frederick my oldest brother is a leader and motivational speaker.

7. Dad have you heard of this alternative group?

8. When did Francesca my cousin have the time to write a book?

9. Before drawing her brother cleaned his messy room.

10. When she fell down the shaggy dog licked her face.

11. I saw the movie *The Diary of Anne Frank* but I liked the book better.

12. The countries of Italy Mexico France and Russia belong to the United Nations.

13. Our visitor Akiko has returned to her native country Japan.

14. Her birthday June 23 1985 is the same as mine.

Name _____

©1999 by Incentive Publications, Inc.
Nashville, TN.

Building Proofreading Skills in Punctuation

Comma

ACTIVITY: Using all of the previously stated comma rules, proofread the following sentences for errors. Use the correct proofreading symbols (see page 5) to add commas where they are necessary and to delete commas where they are not necessary. Some sentences may not require any punctuation changes.

Sample:

Elizabeth Taylor, was one of the most important movie stars in the 1960s, and now she is a very successful businesswoman in the perfume industry.

1. The famous designer Nell Bennett, will speak today at Macy's at, 3:00 P.M.

2. Since I have not completed my research paper on time Mrs. Slaton has given me three days to finish it.

3. If you will help me bake you may have some cookies.

4. You may work on the computer, for an hour or you may work on the GeoSafari®.

5. Yes Allen the play *Evita* is one written, by Andrew Lloyd Webber.

6. Of course, Lori Sandra would be happy to go with you, to Sears.

7. Walker's favorite sports are, canoeing basketball hiking and swimming.

8. Call me Leland if you can assist at the concession stand.

9. Gustav have you heard of the author Carl Sandburg?

10. We were thirsty and we were hungry.

11. We came to the office early worked hard and left late on Tuesday, of last week.

12. In addition your participation in class discussions, is a part of your grade.

13. By the way have you ordered your cap, and gown for graduation?

14. Please bring to class the following materials: pencil paper ruler colored pencil protractor and your math book.

15. Before Mantoya, started running he looked rather pale, and tired.

16. If it rains, this afternoon we will go to the movies, instead.

Name _____

©1999 by Incentive Publications, Inc.
Nashville, TN.

Building Proofreading Skills in Punctuation

Hyphen and Apostrophe

ACTIVITY: Proofread the following sentences for the correct use of the **hyphen** and **apostrophe.** Using the correct proofreading symbols (see page 5), punctuate the following sentences. If no punctuation is required, write **none** in the left margin.

> **Rule 1:** Use a hyphen to divide a word at the end of a line. (The school's air condi-tioner stopped on the hottest day of the year.)
>
> **Rule 2:** Use a hyphen with compound numbers from twenty-one to ninety-nine and with fractions used as adjectives (a two-thirds majority of the vote).
>
> **Rule 3:** To form the possessive case of a singular noun, add an apostrophe and an s (the dog's bone).
>
> **Rule 4:** To form the possessive case of a plural noun ending in *s*, add an apostrophe and an s (the students**'s** reports). (There are some exceptions to this rule which you will not need to know for this exercise.)
>
> **Rule 5:** Use an apostrophe to show where letters have been omitted in a contraction. (We'll sing several campfire songs.)

Sample:
Did you find the doctors bag in his car?

1. When did the Millers dog run away from home?

2. Isnt that Andrews black cat that I saw in the street?

3. Bobs new car was traveling at seventy five miles per hour.

4. Many animals homes are destroyed when rain forests are cut down.

5. My mother in law lives in the South American country of Bolivia.

6. Its too soon for the childrens toys to be broken.

7. The woodworking book has a beautiful design on its cover.

8. Marianne paid ninety nine cents for a one half pound bag of peanuts.

9. I wonder whether or not the young driver of that red Corvette is going to pre cede us or follow us to the cemetery.

10. Naturally the four cylinder car engine was much faster than the two cylinder one.

11. The current president and vice president won reelection by a three fourths majority.

BONUS:

Write five sentences with mistakes using hyphens and apostrophes. Then give your paper to a classmate to proofread.

Name _____

Building Proofreading Skills in Punctuation

Semicolon and Colon

ACTIVITY: Proofread the following sentences for the correct usage of the **semicolon** and **colon**. Use the proofreading symbols (see page 5) to add semicolons and hyphens where necessary.

Rule 1: Use a semicolon between independent clauses in a sentence if they are not joined by *and, but, nor, for,* or *yet.*

Rule 2: Use a semicolon between independent clauses joined by such words as *for example, besides, nevertheless, therefore, however,* and *instead.*

Rule 3: A semicolon (rather than a comma) may be needed to separate the independent clauses of a compound sentence if commas appear within the clauses.

Rule 4: Use a colon before a list of items, especially after expressions such as *the following* or *as follows.*

Rule 5: Use a colon between the hour and minute when writing the time.

Rule 6: Use a colon after the salutation of a business letter.

Sample:

The garage, living room, kitchen, and dining room are on the first floor the bedrooms and bathrooms are on the second floor.

1. On our first trip to Disneyworld, we wanted to see Epcot Center my little sister wanted to stay in the Magic Kingdom.

2. Our favorite sights and rides at Disneyworld included the following the Teacups, Magic Mountain, and the Disney Parade.

3. Our family enjoyed many different foods while we visited the Magic Kingdom Mexican, Polynesian, and French.

4. My friends enjoy playing many different games however, we play some games over and over checkers, chess, and video games.

5. I have many favorite songs one of my favorite songs is from the movie *Waiting to Exhale.*

6. We arrived at the party exactly at 8 30 P.M. and left at 11 25 P.M.

7. She disliked so many of her chores cleaning up her room, washing the dishes, emptying the trash, and taking care of her cat.

8. Dear Mrs. Caldwell   Dear Sir   Gentlemen

9. Jay raised horses, cows, and rabbits he really enjoyed caring for the horses.

10. I have never forgotten my grandfather's advice "My son, once you tell one lie, you often have to tell more lies to cover up the first one."

Name _____

©1999 by Incentive Publications, Inc.
Nashville, TN.

Building Proofreading Skills in Punctuation

Quotation Marks and Underlining

ACTIVITY: Proofread the following sentences for the correct usage of **quotation marks** and **underlining (or italics)**. Using the correct proofreading symbols (see page 5), add quotation marks and underlining where necessary.

> **Rule 1:** Use underlining (or *italics*) for titles of books, periodicals, works of art, plays, films, ships, and the like.
>
> **Rule 2:** Use quotation marks to enclose a direct quotation (a person's exact words).
>
> **Rule 3:** A direct quotation is set off from the rest of the sentence by commas or by a question mark or exclamation point.
>
> **Rule 4:** A period or a comma following a quotation should be placed *inside* the closing quotation marks. A period is only used if the quotation comes at the end of the sentence that includes it.
>
> **Rule 5:** A question mark or an exclamation point should be placed *inside* the closing quotation marks if the quotation is a question or an exclamation. Otherwise, it should be placed *outside* the closing quotation marks.
>
> **Rule 6:** Use quotation marks to enclose titles of short works (poems, short stories, songs, television programs, and articles).

Sample:

Marcia replied, I couldn't read the book, The Friendship, because my dog ate it.

1. Did you see that beautiful hot air balloon? called Francis.

2. Jurassic Park by Michael Crichton is one of my favorite books.

3. My mother said angrily, Get your hair cut today or suffer the consequences!

4. Have you read Call of the Wild by Jack London, Pierre asked, the story of a dog and a boy?

5. All of my friends really enjoyed the article Denzel Washington, The Movie Star, in the recent issue of Ebony.

6. Blaine, Tiffany, and Matt all exclaimed, Planet Hollywood is so awesome!

7. Zachary told us in confidence that he was afraid of ghost stories.

8. Robert Frost's poem Stopping By the Woods on a Snowy Evening is one of my favorites.

9. Yes, Ms. McCoy, I did cheat on my math test that we took last week on Chapter 11, said Juanita.

10. Six Flags over Texas, said Barbara, has many exciting rides and attractions.

11. On our trip to Paris, we visited the Louvre where we saw the Mona Lisa; the most exciting part of our trip was when we returned on the Queen Elizabeth II.

Name _____

Building Proofreading Skills in Punctuation

Cumulative Review

Spelling, Capitalization, and Punctuation

ACTIVITY: Proofread the following letter for errors in **spelling, capitalization,** and **punctuation**. Use the proofreading symbols (see page 5) to correct spelling and capitalization errors and to add or delete punctuation where necessary. Some sentences may not require any corrections.

2917 Bristol Way N.E.
Atlanta Georgia 30309.
Septamber, 12 1996

Mrs Lawanda Greene President
Acme Publishing Company
448 Larchment Boulevard
Baton Rouge Lousana. 70805

Dear Mrs Greene

We will be delighted to welcome your neice Marlene as one of our writer's when she moves to Atlanta as you outlined in your recent letter Marlenes background in creative writing sounds extremly encouraging for our new series of books entitled Mysteries of the World. When you said, Marlene was one of the most dynamic writers in her class of seventy five students, I was most impresed. We all feel fortunuate to have Marlene join our team of writers'.

To speed the process of imployment records for our Human Resources department please ask Marlene to complete the following aplication state and federal frorms, insurance forms and documentation forms. could you ask her to also bring her social security card, so that we will be able to make a copy of it.

Our entire staff at Bristol Publishing looks forward to greeting Marlene.

Sincerly

Constance Bristol President

CB/tm

Building Proofreading Skills in Punctuation

Cumulative Review

Spelling, Capitalization, and Punctuation

ACTIVITY: Proofread the following report, "The Universe" by Conrad Lisco, for errors in **spelling, capitalization,** and **punctuation.** Use the proofreading symbols (see page 5) to correct all errors.

The Universe
by Conrad Lisco

have you ever wundered what is out in the unievrse there are things out there that we have never seen things that are just waiting to be discovered there may be new plants stars moons or evan more galexis

before tecnology was imporved people thoght the Stars wer jest shinin objects in the sky the ancient roman and greek civilixations made up wunderful mythes about gods and goddesses they were suposedly responsable for creating the universe and the vareus constalatoins were named after them as were the planets galileo was able to develap a quite simple Telscope by first making a "spyglass" similar to the ones that were around in 1608 in 1610 galileo was able to see the plant jupiter and som of its moons even with his Telscope the stars and most planetts were quiet out of reech at that time the peple of the seventeenth century thought that galileos telscope was a graat inventon

much later Scientists invented new ways to Discover the stars philosopheers devellped theories and many new ideas arose still people could not totally understand the universe the moon and other planets were now coming closer into view?

since the launching of sputnik (means "travelling companion" in russian) in 1957 many changes have taken place now we have great mashines and paople who can acomplish grat feats in science there are Space Shuttles like the challenger sattelites such as voyager and the Space station Mir (means "peace" in russian)! today we can say that we have gotten a closer look at the universe than ever befor

in conclusion over the years people hav strugled to unlock the Mysteries of the universe still today "we strive for the stars and dream of Space travel" to the planets in our Solar System and others.

Name _____

©1999 by Incentive Publications, Inc.
Nashville, TN.

Building Proofreading Skills in Punctuation

Cumulative Review

Spelling, Capitalization, and Punctuation

ACTIVITY: Proofread the following poem, "A Poison Tree" by William Blake. Using the proofreading symbols (see page 5), correct all errors in **spelling, capitalization, and punctuation.**

A Poison Tree
by William Blake

I was angry with my freind:
I told my rath, my wrath did end.
i was angry with my foe:
I told it not my wrath did grow.

And i watered it in fears,
night and morning with my tears;
And I suned it with smiles,
And with soft deceitfull wiles.

And it grew both day and niht,
Til it bore an Apple bright.
And my foe beheld it shin,
And he knew that it was myne.

and into my garden stole
When the night, had veiled the pole;*
In the Morning glad i see
My foe outstretced beneath the tree.

*pole: sky

Name

©1999 by Incentive Publications, Inc.
Nashville, TN.

Building Proofreading Skills in Punctuation
Cumulative Review
Punctuation and Capitalization

ACTIVITY: Proofread the following school announcement for errors in **punctuation** and **capitalization.** Use the proofreading symbols (see page 5) to correct the mistakes. Copy the corrected announcement on a separate piece of paper.

INTERNATIONAL CELEBRATION

Parents and Friends of briarcliff middle school, we cordially invite you to celebrate our Third Annual International Dinner on march 15 1997? This celebration of our Cultural Diversity involves an entire week to honor our heritage from many lands many backgrounds and many languages!

Last year when the PTA led us in a festival of redecoration we hung flags and banners from twenty one different countries. many classes decorated flags to honor countries they had studied. Families also sponsored or purchased flags to honor their home-lands, and their new school. In almost every class students learned interesting facts about each country, and studied the language of a particular country.

For this years week long celebration we invite parents and friends to participate in one of the following ways teach a craft, cook a special dish, share or teach a dance, or speak to individual classes about your homeland If you are interested in helping please contact Marilyn Van derber at (440) 741-1234 after 700 P.M.

Join us for our Third Annual International Dinner on March 15 1997 at 6:00 P.M. in the Briarcliff Middle School Cafeteria. Families should bring dishes from their homelands. The pta will provide the soft drinks and paper products. Our keynote speaker will be the well known storyteller Carmen Fiedlo. For reservations please call Dr Theodore Washburn at (440) 741-7890 before March 10, 1997.

SPECIAL NOTE: There are about 35 corrections needed in the above announcement. Did you find all of the errors? If not, reread the announcement to see if you can find the errors you missed.

Name

Chapter 4

Building Proofreading Skills in Language Usage

This chapter will provide practice in proofreading for language usage. Although the traditional rules for language usage often seem unnecessarily rigid, grammar plays a more important role than many people think. You as a student can forget a comma once in a while without doing any harm to your writing. However, some mistakes in grammar are so apparent and distracting that any knowledgeable reader will notice them immediately.

Each activity in this chapter presents exercises to provide proofreading practice in the following areas: parts of speech, subject-verb agreement, sentence fragments, run-on sentences, pronoun and antecedent agreement, dangling and misplaced modifiers, comparison of adjectives and adverbs, and double negatives. Working through the following activities will improve your proofreading skills as well as your skills in writing and self-expression.

REVIEWING THE PARTS OF SPEECH

- A **noun** is a word that names a person, place, thing, or idea (doctor, Wyoming, book, and honesty).

- A **pronoun** is a word used in place of one or more nouns (her, its, their, someone, mine, those, none, and myself).

- A **verb** is a word that expresses action or otherwise helps to make a statement (has, shall, would, jump, worry, earn, think, shout, toss, disturb, and considered).

- An **adjective** is a word used to modify a noun or a pronoun (the, better, beautiful, this, many, last, and eager). *Hint:* Usually an adjective comes in front of a noun.

- An **adverb** is a word used to modify a verb, an adjective, or another adverb. An adverb usually answers one of these questions: *Where? When? How? To what extent? (too, very, nearby, promptly, never, suddenly, carefully, angrily,* and *down). Hint:* Many adverbs end in -ly.

- A **preposition** is a word used to show the relationship of a noun or pronoun to some other word in the sentence (under, after, with, in, beside, at, by, and between).

- A **conjunction** is a word that joins words or groups of words (and, but, or, nor, for, yet, and so).

- An **interjection** is a word that expresses strong feeling or sudden emotion and is not related grammatically to other words in the sentence (hey, wow, ouch, stop, oh, yes, well, great, and surprise). *Hint:* Interjections may be followed by an exclamation point (Hey! Watch out for that speeding car).

©1999 by Incentive Publications, Inc.
Nashville, TN.

Building Proofreading Skills in Language Usage

Parts of Speech

ACTIVITY: Proofread the following list of **adjectives, nouns, verbs, adverbs, prepositions, conjunctions,** and **interjections.** Each item below gives four possible choices for the part of speech listed. Choose the word that is an example of the **part of speech** listed in the first column. Circle the letter of the correct answer.

Sample:

adjective	a. softest (circled)	b. tightly	c. quickly	d. against

1. **adverb**	a. haunted	b. catching	c. ouch	d. slightly
2. **preposition**	a. what	b. quietly	c. between	d. approach
3. **conjunction**	a. but	b. goodness	c. below	d. are
4. **interjection**	a. drove	b. noisily	c. oops	d. uncertain
5. **verb**	a. growth	b. tulip	c. she	d. wishing
6. **adjective**	a. reach	b. vacant	c. quarrel	d. girl
7. **adverb**	a. clearly	b. clear	c. nor	d. without
8. **conjunction**	a. any	b. several	c. would	d. and
9. **preposition**	a. round	b. around	c. distant	d. running
10. **pronoun**	a. wish	b. Rocky	c. him	d. wishing
11. **noun**	a. swimsuit	b. swam	c. splashed	d. soapy
12. **adjective**	a. bought	b. belong	c. bother	d. beautiful
13. **pronoun**	a. there	b. their	c. three	d. thus
14. **preposition**	a. aboard	b. board	c. bored	d. abound
15. **verb**	a. slippery	b. studious	c. prepared	d. conductor
16. **adjective**	a. over	b. from	c. several	d. cartoon
17. **interjection**	a. wonder	b. greatly	c. visited	d. goodness

Name _____

©1999 by Incentive Publications, Inc.
Nashville, TN.

Building Proofreading Skills in Language Usage

Troublesome Verbs (sit and set; rise and raise; lie and lay)

ACTIVITY: Carefully proofread the following sentences for errors in using the six **troublesome verbs (sit** and **set; rise** and **raise; lie** and **lay)**. Decide if the italicized verb has been used correctly in the sentence. If it has not, use the proofreading symbols (see page 5) to correct the verb.

> **Rule 1:** Use a form of **sit (sit, sat, sitting)** when you mean "to rest in a sitting position." *(She **sat** patiently waiting for the Olympic runners.)* Use a form of **set (set, sets, setting)** when you mean "to put or place" something. *(Kennedy **set** the dinner table for four special guests.)*

> **Rule 2:** Use a form of **rise (rise, rose, risen)** when you mean "to ascend, to swell up, and to rise in value or force." *(We waited for the dough to **rise**.)* Use a form of **raise (raise, raised, raised)** when you mean "to lift up, to cause it to go up, or to increase in amount." *(Stanley **raised** the flag.)*

> **Rule 3:** Use a form of **lie (lie, lay, lain, lying)** when you mean "to rest or recline." *(Susanna has been **lying** on the chaise lounge all afternoon.)* Use a form of **lay (lay, laid, laying)** when you mean "to put or place" something. *(Josephine has been **laying** bathroom tiles in a unique pattern.)*

Sample:
By early morning Nikki had ~~rose~~ *risen* high in his hot air balloon.

1. You may borrow my thesaurus, which is *laying* on the floor next to the sofa.

2. Mother asked Sandra to *sat* the table before the guests arrived.

3. Because Tommy has been sick, he must *lay* down and rest for one hour.

4. She thought that she had *lain* the briefcase on the front seat of her car.

5. After we had been *setting* there for almost an hour, we learned the bus had left us.

6. Scarlet carefully *lay* out the gown that she was wearing to the dance.

7. After a delicious dinner, we *set* down to play a trivia game.

8. The distinguished speaker slowly *raised* to the podium.

9. Fabio was *lying* the tiles in the new bathroom.

10. When I walked past the office, Tommy was *setting* in the chair next to the principal.

12. Many of my classmates have *laid* awake at night after reading one of Poe's stories.

Name _____

©1999 by Incentive Publications, Inc.
Nashville, TN.

Building Proofreading Skills in Language Usage

Subject-Verb Agreement

ACTIVITY: Proofread the following sentences for errors in **subject-verb agreement.** Use the proofreading symbols (see page 5) to correct the verb in each sentence.

> **Rule:** The subject and verb of a sentence must agree in number. A singular subject requires a singular verb, and a plural subject requires a plural verb.
> Singular: *The state **bird** of Georgia **is** the Brown Thrasher.*
> Plural: *The **candidates have** all qualified for the upcoming election.*

Sample:

The hamster ~~were~~ *was* in his cage all night long.

1. Marvin and Lillian visits New York every spring.

2. Peoria, Illinois are a wonderful, quiet place to raise a family.

3. The majority of the Russian voters is voting in the presidential election today.

4. The dark-haired girl were chosen for the Miss America contest in her local pageant.

5. The cherry tomatoes in my dad's garden grows rapidly.

6. My new black cocker spaniel run away every time I call him.

7. The palm trees on the Caribbean island sways in the wind all day long.

8. The experienced pitcher throw the ball in a variety of ways.

9. The beautifully colored macaw have an extremely powerful beak.

10. The assistant principal of our school award certificates for attendance.

11. The Aztecs was conquered by the Spanish after much bloodshed.

12. She lie on the dirty floor of the newly renovated basement.

13. The candidate shake hands with as many voters as she can.

BONUS:

Write a passage in which some subjects and verbs do not agree; then, give it to a classmate to proofread.

Name _____

©1999 by Incentive Publications, Inc.
Nashville, TN.

Building Proofreading Skills in Language Usage

Sentence Fragments

ACTIVITY: Proofread the following for **sentence fragments.** (Remember that fragments are pieces of sentences punctuated as if they were complete sentences.) Circle **S** if the group of words is a complete sentence, or circle **F** if the group of words is a fragment. Then, rewrite the fragments to make complete sentences.

   Rule: A sentence is a clause that forms a complete thought.

Sample:

   S Ⓕ   Wimbledon, one of the most important tennis tournaments. ,begins Saturday

1. S   F   Ms. Moody told her class to divide into small groups.

2. S   F   Coretta Scott King, the widow of Dr. Martin Luther King.

3. S   F   While Terry was on vacation, his car caused him a lot of trouble.

4. S   F   As I was slowly driving home from the movies.

5. S   F   Having been given the signal to start the games.

6. S   F   His older sisters always treated him so cruelly.

7. S   F   Waiting patiently at the dentist office for several hours.

8. S   F   I simply do not understand why he does not go to the doctor.

9. S   F   When we moved last summer to San Diego.

10. S   F   Please open your books to page 115.

11. S   F   At the bottom of page 115, you will notice two exercises.

12. S   F   Who always complain about the cafeteria meals.

13. S   F   Offering additional classes in Spanish for all seventh-graders.

14. S   F   Learning to operate a computer is quite an accomplishment.

15. S   F   Josh considered running for seventh-grade president.

BONUS:

Write a paragraph containing several sentence fragments. Give it to a classmate to proof-read and correct.

Name _____

©1999 by Incentive Publications, Inc.
Nashville, TN.

Building Proofreading Skills in Language Usage

Pronoun-Antecedent Agreement

ACTIVITY: Every **pronoun** refers to another word, which is called its **antecedent.** Whenever you use a pronoun, make sure that it agrees with its antecedent in number and gender.

Proofread the following sentences for errors in **pronoun–antecedent agreement.** Use the proofreading symbols (see page 5) for omitting and inserting a word to correct the sentences. Some sentences may not need any corrections.

Sample:

Everyone in Mrs. Slaton's class gave ~~their~~ *his or her* report on space exploration.

1. No one on the committee gave their approval on the upcoming issue.

2. Each of the newspapers has had the governor's picture on its front page.

3. Several others, including Ben, volunteered to present his first.

4. The science book had Bryan's name written inside their cover.

5. Neither the father nor the son had remembered to bring its tool kit.

6. Nobody in the fifth period class would admit to their low test score.

7. In most cases, a cat or a dog that becomes lost in the deep woods can easily take care of themselves.

8. Nadia and Keshia wore her cheerleader uniforms to the practice today.

9. A few of my neighbors have installed watering systems in their yards.

10. One of my goofy relatives always wears their tennis shoes without strings.

Name _____

©1999 by Incentive Publications, Inc.
Nashville, TN.

Building Proofreading Skills in Language Usage

Run-On Sentences

ACTIVITY: Run-on sentences are two or more sentences that "run together" without a period separating them. Remember, run-on sentences sometimes have commas separating them.
Proofread the following passage for run-on sentences. Use the proofreading symbols (see page 5) to correct the run-ons. Remember to start each new sentence with a capital letter and to end each with the proper punctuation mark.

Sample: There are five themes of geography one of the themes is *location.*

Location refers to the position of people and places on the earth's surface, the exact position or absolute location of something on the earth's surface can be identified by using lines of longitude and latitude. Relative location is the relationship of one place to other places people think about such relationships when they decide where to live, where to work, or where to build a school.

Another geographic theme is *place* three fundamental characteristics give identity to a place and distinguish it from other places: physical characteristics, human characteristics, and image. Physical characteristics include landforms, bodies of water, climate, soils, natural vegetation, and animal life. Human characteristics, however, include buildings, farms, and other human environments that people create.

Human-environment interaction is another geographic theme different people use the natural environment in different ways people often modify the natural environment to meet their needs, when humans interact with the natural environment, consequences always exist some are intended others are not.

Relationships between people in different places constitute the fourth geographic theme, *movement*—the movement of people, goods, and ideas people travel from one place to another often people in one place have goods that people in another place want. The people in these two places are potential trading partners.

A *region,* the fifth and final geographic theme, is an area that has some unifying characteristics, they are convenient and manageable for organizing our knowledge of the world there are many ways to define a region, depending on the issues or problems being considered. The criteria used to define regions can be physical, human, or both.

Name

Building Proofreading Skills in Language Usage

Dangling and Misplaced Modifiers

ACTIVITY: A **dangling** or **misplaced modifier** changes the meaning of a sentence and makes it unclear or nonsensical because the modifying phrase is located in the wrong place. Proofread the following sentences to find the **dangling** and **misplaced modifiers.** First, underline the dangling or misplaced modifier. Then, use the proofreading circles, arrows, and transpose symbols (see page 5) to show where the phrase belongs. You may need to add or change some words and to correct capitalization and punctuation, as well.

Sample:

At the age of six, Foluke's mom took him to the zoo. (tr)

1. Pacing the floor angrily my cellular phone was ringing.

2. Many people often avoid walking under ladders who are superstitious.

3. I saw Dontavius Lott run fifty yards for a touchdown while eating a hot dog and drinking a coke.

4. Isaac thought about his problems riding a bicycle and singing a song.

5. Staying at the beach house all summer, the sun-block supply was depleted.

6. After walking up the hill, the bucket had to be lowered into the well.

7. Father baked a two-layer cake for the birthday party that was dripping strawberry frosting.

8. The audience gave a standing ovation when Deontae finished his piano performance in the balcony.

9. The acorns were crushed by the tractor lying on the ground.

10. The typist finished her work and began to drive home at her desk.

11. Swimming perfectly, a gold medal was won by Amy at the Summer Olympics in Atlanta.

BONUS:

Write several sentences in which the word order sounds wrong or makes the meaning unclear. First, proofread the sentences yourself to be sure that each can be corrected. Then, give the uncorrected sentences to a classmate to proofread.

Name _____

Building Proofreading Skills in Language Usage

Comparitive Forms of Adjectives and Adverbs

ACTIVITY: Proofread the following sentences for errors in the **comparitive forms of adjectives and adverbs.** Use the proofreading symbols (see page 5) to rewrite the adjective or adverb, using the correct degree of comparison.

>   **Rule 1:** When you are comparing two things (*comparative degree*), add the suffix **-er** to most one-syllable modifiers *(stronger).* If the modifier has two or more syllables, then use the word **more** or **less** *(more clever, less likely).*

>   **Rule 2:** When you are comparing three or more things (*superlative degree*), add the suffix **-est** to most one-syllable modifiers *(warmest).* If the modifier has two or more syllables, then use the word **most** or **least** *(most dependable, least reliable).*

Sample:
That was the ~~greater~~ **greatest** movie I have ever seen.

1. The magician had to perform the difficultest magic tricks of all the performers.

2. The magician's assistant, Maria, was the more beautiful of all the performers in the show.

3. The second act of the show was the less exciting of all the performances.

4. Children seemed to enjoy the performance of the bears better of all.

5. Special effects were used effectively than they were previously.

6. Lynn completed her science project earliest than anyone else in her class.

7. For the Invent America Contest, Tom created the more fascinating creations.

8. This math problem was the difficulter of all the problems we've had this year.

9. The lion is considered to be one of the most fierce animal in the grassland of Kenya.

10. She worked hardest than the other mechanic at the automotive center.

Name _____

©1999 by Incentive Publications, Inc.
Nashville, TN.

Building Proofreading Skills in Language Usage

Double Negatives

ACTIVITY: Words such as *no, not, none, never, no one, nothing, scarcely,* and *hardly* are called **negatives.** (Many negatives begin with the letter **n.**) Negative statements in standard English require only one negative word. Use of more than one negative word is called a **double negative.** *(We do* not *have* no *homework for tomorrow.)* Always avoid the use of double negatives.

Using the proofreading symbol for deleting (see page 5), first delete the double negative. Then rewrite each sentence correctly on the line provided.

Sample:

Too much homework doesn't ~~scarcely~~ leave time to watch television.

Too much homework doesn't leave time to watch television.

1. Rosie said, "I don't want no one on my show with a bad attitude."

   _____

2. Your answer to the math problem doesn't make no sense to me.

   _____

3. I don't know nothing about our state's history or its government.

   _____

4. George hasn't never been to the Black Hills of South Dakota.

   _____

5. The candidate told the reporters that she would not have no comment.

   _____

6. Johnny's mother could not hardly believe she had won the state lottery.

   _____

7. Don't never use "none" and "nothing" in the same sentence.

   _____

8. I didn't receive no notice about my failing grade in English.

   _____

BONUS:

Write several sentences using double negatives. Then, exchange your paper with a classmate to proofread.

Name _____

Building Proofreading Skills in Language Usage
Cumulative Review
Spelling, Capitalization, Punctuation, and Language Usage

ACTIVITY: Correct the errors in spelling, capitalization, punctuation, subject-verb agreement, sentence fragments, run-on sentences, dangling and misplaced modifiers, and double negatives from Isabelle McCoy's true story, "The Day of the Bubbles." Use the proofreading symbols (see page 5) to make your corrections.

The Day of the Bubbles

when my brother edward were a young boy only about four he folowed my Mom around as she did her work We lived in a two story house with a full basement in the basement was the washing machine and a large play area. My brother would play while my mom worked with his train and other toys.

One day while she was doing the laundrey and working on supper upstairs my bother obvoiusly became borred and wanted to try something knew? He got the box of detergeant and was going to use it for who know what! it spiled and there were detergeant all over the floor. Seeing the mess and not wanting to get into troble. My brother naturelly did what any four-year old would do. He tryed to cover it up but it was a large spill. he look for the broom but it was not in sight. What he did see was the hose that my mom used to scrubb the floor of the basment? Now my brother had wached my mom do this many times. So he decided he wanted to wash the floor he got the hose and turned on the water. Unfortunately, he turned on the water full blast and there write before his eyes a mound of sope bubbles began to form. Wow he said. This is great—bubbles, just like in the bathtub, but no bath.

Name _____

The Day of the Bubbles, continued

he of course promtly forgot that he was trying not to get in trouble for spiling the detergeant. Edward begins to slip and slide through the bubbles. His squiels of delight carrried upstairs to the kitchen. Mom went to the head of the stairs and called to my brother, What are you doing. His reply was just what you or I would say if we were caught doing something wrong.

He said, I'm not doing nothing, Mommy.

My mother, being the inteligant person that she is, didnt beleive him for an instant she proceeded to investtigate. reaching the bottom step, giggling and the sound of water running she heard. As mom turned the corner, she was just in time to see my brother standing ammid a large mound of bubbles. Needless to say my mom was not to happy her roast was cooking and my dad would be home soon. She did not have no time to deal with this mess.

Mother said, "Edward come hear?

Like an "ideal" four year old caught being bad, he replied, "No!

My mom was very angry. And took a step toward my brother She didn't realise that the floor would be so slippery and her feet went out from under her. Mom slides across the floor, feet first. Edward thought she was joining in on the fun, and He slides the other way. After trying to catch him several times mom stoped and sat on the floor! My brother made another slide trough the bubbles and landed in her lap. by this time my mothers' angry had turned to laghter.

©1999 by Incentive Publications, Inc.
Nashville, TN.

Chapter 5

Proofreading for Clarity, Transition, and Order

By now you have learned to proofread for a variety of errors: spelling, capitalization, punctuation, parts of speech, subject-verb agreement, sentence fragments, run-on sentences, dangling and misplaced modifiers, comparison of adjectives and adverbs, pronoun-antecedent agreement, and double negatives. The lessons in this chapter involve more sophisticated material on paragraphing, word order, transitions, sentence variety, wordiness, and writing effective sentences. Each activity will give you practice in all areas of proofreading, thus, helping you write any assignment more successfully.

ACTIVITY: Review of proofreading marks. In the space next to each proofreading mark, write what the mark means. Then, on the second line, give an example of how the symbol is used.

Sample:

b̲̲   *Capitalize a lowercase letter*

Example: *be on time for cheerleading practice.*
         ̲̲

↗ 1. _____

Example: _____

⌒ 2. _____

Example: _____

ℬ 3. _____

Example: _____

⊙ 4. _____

Example: _____

∿ 5. _____

Example: _____

Name _____

©1999 by Incentive Publications, Inc.
Nashville, TN.

Proofreading for Clarity, Transition, and Order

Review of Proofreading Marks, Continued

₧ 6. _____

Example: _____

∨ or ∧ 7. _____

Example: _____

∶| 8. _____

Example: _____

(tr) 9. _____

Example: _____

ℓ 10. _____

Example: _____

11. _____

Example: _____

"∨ ∨" 12. _____

Example: _____

(sp) 13. _____

Example: _____

(stet) 14. _____

Example: _____

∨̓ 15. _____

Example: _____

Name _____

©1999 by Incentive Publications, Inc.
Nashville, TN.

Proofreading for Clarity, Transition, and Order

Sentence Order

ACTIVITY: When we write, it is important to make sure that our ideas are written in a sensible order. In the following paragraphs, the sentences are **out of order.** Edit the order of the sentences by writing the number *1* at the beginning of what should be the first sentence, the number *2* at the beginning of the second sentence, and so on. In case you change your mind, use a pencil so that you can erase. When you have finished, read the sentences aloud in the order in which you have renumbered them. Finally, write the three paragraphs on a clean sheet of paper.

Remember: A paragraph should begin with a **topic sentence** that tells the general idea of the paragraph.

1. The Egyptians had stools, chairs, chests, tables, and beds, examples of which can be seen in museums today. They also painted scenes of everyday life on the walls of the tombs. Many centuries later, when the sealed tombs were opened, examples of both the real furniture and the furniture painted on the walls were found. The origin of furniture as we know it goes back to ancient Egypt. They put such everyday objects in their tombs. Some of these were indoor scenes that showed an abundance of furniture.

2. In fact, these contests were often the main events at country fairs. We all know the story of Robin Hood and his band of merry archers who roamed Sherwood Forest. The sport of archery has long been associated with tales of romance and valor. We know, too, of William Tell, whose skill with a bow saved his life. Many a tale set in early England tells of picturesque and colorful archery contests.

3. About sixty years later, a railroad connected the two cities, and, by the twentieth century, fast planes and automobiles had been developed. By 1775, horse-drawn coaches had lessened the time to two days. In less than three hundred years, the ever-increasing speed of travel has completely changed our ideas of distance. In 1675, the normal way to travel from New York City to Philadelphia was on foot, and the trip took three to five days. Now we can cover the distance in a few minutes by jet.

Name _____

©1999 by Incentive Publications, Inc.
Nashville, TN.

Proofreading for Clarity, Transition, and Order

Sentence Order, Continued

4. Today, over twenty-two billion tin cans are used to store packed food. As long ago as 55 B.C., the early Romans coated copper vessels with tin to make them suitable as food containers. A tin can, first of all, has very little tin in it. Everyone uses tin cans, but few people know much about them. Coating a metal with tin is a process that has been known a long time. The can is made of tin plate that is over 98% steel with only a coating of tin.

5. There are three important actions that students can take to save energy. For example, I noticed a newspaper article last week about opening a bus lane on Decatur Street. Last evening at home, I counted five lights that were left on needlessly. We should support this idea in our letters. At home, we can turn off lights that are not in use. Finally, when we travel to the mall, to the skating rink, or to other places with friends, we should use public transportation, such as buses, subways, and trains. At school, we can write letters to public officials, reminding them of how important it is to conserve energy whenever possible. I promptly turned them off.

Name _____

Proofreading for Clarity, Transition, and Order

Word Order within Sentences

ACTIVITY: Writers often change the order of words in sentences to make the meaning clearer. Often they edit to make a sentence flow more effectively. To do this, writers use proofreading symbols such as circles, arrows, transpose marks, and so forth (see page 5).

Proofread the sentences below and correct them by using the appropriate proofreading symbols. You may need to add or delete words.

Sample:

I read about the lost kitten that was found in today's newspaper.

1. Pass me the mashed potatoes and gravy, please.

2. We saw the trapeze artist swinging dangerously through our binoculars.

3. Coming in for a landing, the air traffic controller radioed the plane.

4. Jogging down the sidewalk my puppy followed me.

5. My toddler crawled into my lap reading a book.

6. To read books in the media center is a wonderful place.

7. The lake the students ate their picnic lunch down by.

8. My married brother Joseph came for the weekend to see me who lives in Wyoming.

9. The jacket belongs to my best friend that I have lost.

10. Walking through Central Park, the chipmunks chattered at me.

11. Our family watched the snow pile up in drifts inside our warm home.

12. Destroyed by the fire, the man looked sadly at the charred house.

13. The messenger gave Mr. Holland two dozen balloons who was dressed as a duck.

14. We quietly tiptoed over the ice in our heavy boots, which had begun to crack.

BONUS:

Write at least four sentences in which the word order is unclear or sounds incorrect. Proofread them yourself to make sure that the sentences can be rewritten. Then, give the incorrect sentences to a classmate to proofread.

Name _____

©1999 by Incentive Publications, Inc.
Nashville, TN.

Proofreading for Clarity, Transition, and Order

Transition

ACTIVITY: Many writers fail to take the reader smoothly from one idea to the next. Moving from one idea to the next is called **transition.** The most commonly used transitional words are: *as, since, because, after, before, next, then, also, however, although, therefore, after, and, but, for ,also, so, while,* and *thus.*

Proofread the following paragraph, and use the proofreading symbols (see page 5) to add the appropriate transitional words where necessary. You may combine sentences and add words if needed. Then, on a separate sheet of paper, rewrite the corrected paragraph.

Sample:

Our Persian cat is quite finicky. She eats only albacore tuna.
; therefore,

Our Persian cat is quite finicky; therefore, she eats only albacore tuna.

The beekeeper had a clever way of finding wild bees. He was carrying a small wooden box with a sliding cover. He would go to a meadow. He would find a bee in a flower and capture it in his box. He would pull back the cover and release the bee. He knew that the pollen-laden insect would return to the tree where the wild bees were gathered. He would carefully record the direction of flight. He would move to the other side of the meadow. He would capture another bee. He would release it. He would record the direction in which it flew. He knew that both bees would head home by the most direct route. He knew that the cluster of bees must be found at the point where his imaginary lines crossed. It was easy to capture the swarm in a large net and move it to his own orchard. The beekeeper was simply using mathematics.

Name

©1999 by Incentive Publications, Inc.
Nashville, TN.

Proofreading for Clarity, Transition, and Order

Sentence Variety

ACTIVITY: When we write, most of us have a problem with stringing together too many words and ideas into a single sentence. Most good writers will include a variety of sentences—some long and some short. One of the best suggestions to follow is to *read aloud* what you have written.

In the following exercise, you are the editor. Using the proofreading symbols, edit the passage below to create sentence variety. You will need to add and delete words as well as change punctuation and capitalization. Then, on a separate sheet of paper, rewrite the corrected paragraph.

Sample:

Dr. Harris Bergman spoke to the audience. ~~He spoke~~ with great conviction.

**With great conviction, Dr. Harris Bergman spoke to the**
**audience.**

Marie and Ellen had colds when they visited their aunt in Hollywood but they remember the stay as a very exciting time, for they took an afternoon bus tour past the big homes of the movie stars, they shopped on Hollywood Boulevard—they couldn't come home without presents for the family—and then Marie went alone to see a live television talk show, and Ellen spent a day in bed to shake off her cold, but the next day Marie stayed in bed for the same reason, and Ellen went to a crowded movie premiere at Grauman's Chinese Theater, and on to the last day of their visit their aunt took them to Disneyland.

Name _____

©1999 by Incentive Publications, Inc.
Nashville, TN.

Proofreading for Clarity, Transition, and Order

Wordiness

ACTIVITY: Writers often use needless extra words—this is called **wordiness.** As you proofread, make your writing crisper and, therefore, more interesting by deleting unnecessary words. In the following passage, delete any extra words by using the proper proofreading symbols. You may even want to delete several needless words and replace them with only one word.

Sample:

I like to think of my brother as a genius because he scored an 800 on the math section of the SAT and he went to Harvard and he scored an 800 on the verbal section.

Not Born a Genius
by Kemit Finch

In order for you to become a genius, you have to work for it because you are not born with a gift that lets you know everything there is to know instantly; however, you can be born with a high IQ and still not be a genius. A classic example is Albert Einstein, who could be called a genius, but he had to work at it. If you want to be a genius, you have to set your goal on it.

I read a story about this "brain child" who was writing computer programs when he was only four years old so he must have been talking at three months of age and I think the title for him is "kid genius." I don't think he was born knowing everything, but he just had a very, very high IQ.

In my opinion, a genius is someone who has very high intellect and a better understanding of the world, but there is no doubt in my mind that a person has to work hard to become a genius. One of the smartest inventors, for instance Benjamin Franklin, performed poorly in school, but he invented many things. It is a fact that very many intelligent people perform very poorly in their academic work.

In summary, there are no guarantees that you will without a doubt become a genius even though you may have a notably extremely high IQ.

Name

Building Proofreading Skills

58

©1999 by Incentive Publications, Inc.
Nashville, TN.

Proofreading for Clarity, Transition, and Order

Combining Sentences

ACTIVITY: Some writers string too many words and ideas together in one sentence. Good writing is composed of a variety of effective sentences—some long and some short. Sentences should not just "bump along;" instead, sentences should "flow" smoothly from word to word, phrase to phrase, and idea to idea. Writing effective sentences will make you a more proficient, successful writer.

Create more effective sentences for the items below by rewriting the sentences according to the directions given for each.

Sample:

During half time, Coach Williams gave the players confidence in themselves. The players were deeply discouraged. *(Combine the two sentences into one by adding an adjective.)*

> ***During halftime, Coach Williams gave the***
> ***discouraged players confidence in themselves.***

1. Heather will not be at the party tomorrow. Brittany will not be there either. *(Combine the two sentences by writing one sentence with a compound subject.)*

_____

_____

2. Todd held the tent up straight. Matthew hammered down the stakes. *(Combine the two sentences into one sentence by putting one idea into an adverb clause.)*

_____

_____

3. Umar Shah lived in India before moving here. He is our new doctor. *(Combine the two sentences into a single sentence by using an appositive phrase. Place the phrase next to the noun it modifies. Put commas at the beginning and end of the appositive phrase.)*

_____

_____

4. In August, Lindsay visited her grandparents in Orlando. She also toured Universal Studios. *(Combine the two sentences into a single sentence with one subject and a compound verb.)*

_____

_____

5. Christina hurried off the stage. She was grinning from ear to ear. *(Combine the two sentences into one sentence by using a verb phrase.)*

_____

_____

BONUS:

Write several items with at least two or three short, choppy sentences. Then, edit each item into one sentence. Give an unedited version to a classmate to edit.

Name _____

©1999 by Incentive Publications, Inc.
Nashville, TN.

Proofreading for Clarity, Transition, and Order

Cumulative Review
Paragraphing, Word Order, Transitions, Wordiness, and Sentence Variety

ACTIVITY: The following report on Robert Frost contains no errors in spelling, punctuation, or capitalization; however, it does contain errors in **paragraphing, word order, transitions, wordiness,** and **sentence variety.**

Edit the report using the sentence combining methods you have learned. Be careful not to change the meaning of the original report. Use the proofreading symbols to correct all errors. Then, rewrite the corrected report on a separate sheet of paper.

A TRADITIONAL POET, ROBERT FROST

Robert Frost was one of America's leading twentieth-century poets. He was a four-time winner of the Pulitzer Prize. Frost grew up in New England. Many of his poems are about the countryside in winter. His poetry is traditional. It is also experimental and universal. Frost's importance as a poet evolved from the power of particular poems. One poem has been popular with students. The poem is entitled "Stopping by Woods on a Snowy Evening." In this poem a traveler pauses on a journey. The traveler pauses for a moment. The journey is by horse and wagon. The traveler watches the snow. The snow is falling in the woods. The woods are far from the nearest village. People disagree about the poem's meaning. They enjoy it immensely. It touches on a deep truth about life. Frost received an unusual number of literary honors. He also received a range of academic and public honors. Robert Frost unquestionably succeeded in realizing his life's ambition: to write "a few poems that will be hard to get rid of."

Name _____

©1999 by Incentive Publications, Inc.
Nashville, TN.

Chapter 6

Proofreading and Editing Activities for Writing

The activities in this chapter will use all of the proofreading practices previously covered in this book. You will: (a) edit a letter to a pen pal, using correct spelling, capitalization, and punctuation; (b) proofread for errors in language usage in a thank-you letter and a business letter; (c) proofread for clarity, transition, and order in a book report; and (d) edit an outline, a report, and a bibliography using all of the skills of proofreading.

Working through these exercises will improve your proofreading confidence as well as your writing skills.

ACTIVITY: Proofread the following letter to a pen pal, using the proofreading symbols (see page 5) to correct the errors in **spelling, punctuation,** and **capitalization.** Then, copy the corrected letter on a separate sheet of paper.

4356 westwind Drive
Edmond, Ok 73013
Janary 5 1997

Dear Conrad

    I had a wounderful christmas Vacation with my family in Oklahoma city. We spent the Holidays with my Grandmother Our family had so much fun carroling on christmas eve. How did you celebrate your holidays in Munich. I hope your vacation was as enjoyible as mine. School begins tommorrow. I am not looking forword to going back? I have been chosen as class reporter for our School Newspaper. I am woried that I will not have enough time for my schoolwork. Our newspaper is called *The Chatter Box.* Does your school have a newspaper!

    You may be woundering why this letter is typed? My Mother has moved her office to our house. And she is letting me use her computer. are you imppressed? I have learned so much in the last month about computers. Do you have a home-computer. I have inclosed a picture of our neighborhood. Please send me a picture of what Munich looks' like in the Winter. I will write to you again as soon as I here from you.

your pen pal,

Josh

Name _____

©1999 by Incentive Publications, Inc.
Nashville, TN.

Proofreading and Editing Activities for Writing

Proofreading for Errors in Language Usage

ACTIVITY: Proofread the following thank-you note for errors in **language usage,** including **subject-verb agreement, sentence fragments, run-on sentences, double negatives,** and **misplaced modifiers.** Correct the note using the proofreading symbols (see page 5). Then, copy the corrected note on a separate sheet of paper.

---

79 Chuckwagon Trail
Casper, WY 82604
September 5, 1996

Dear Kendall,

Since I returned home. I been thinking about the marvelous week I spent with you and your family in Yellowstone National Park. The park had always been a picture album place to me, and now I have my own photos, but the outdoor scenery were only part of the enjoyment I experienced with your family.

Waking up in the morning to the smell of bacon and eggs, hiking up the steep trails, and sitting around the campfire singing songs. I will long remember all of these things. I will not never forget the morning we were awakened to the sound through our trash cans of the grizzly bear rummaging. What a way to wake up!

Please tell your mother as soon as they are developed I will send her some of the photos. Thanks again for such an enjoyable and relaxing week.

Your friend,

Alexa Rae

To the Teacher: You may choose to make a transparency of this activity for use on the overhead. Then, ask for class participation.

Name _____

©1999 by Incentive Publications, Inc.
Nashville, TN.

Proofreading and Editing Activities for Writing

Proofreading for Errors in Spelling, Capitalization, Punctuation, and Language Usage

ACTIVITY: Proofread the following book report on *The Witch of Blackbird Pond* for errors in spelling, capitalization, punctuation, subject-verb agreement, run-on sentences, sentence fragments, and paragraphing. Use the appropriate proofreading symbols (see page 5) to correct the report.

The Witch of Blackbird Pond
Thomas Ashley McCoy IV

The Witch of Blackbird Pond by Elizabeth George Speare, a famous author of other historicial novels. This enjoyable, entertaining book, first published in 1958, is a newbery award winner.

The story take place during the Nine-teenth century in Connecticut Colony. The main character is Katherine Tyler, also known as "Kit" this fictional book has many other interesting characters, especially Hannah, an old widow who becomes a close friend of Kit. Kit sails on a ship called the Dolphin to Wetherfield, a town in Connecticut, leaving the Carribean Islands. With no one to turn to she hopes that her only living relatives will accept her Kit finds herself in a strange and lonely place quite different from the sunny Caribbean Islands where she once lived. In the strict Puritan community home of her relatives. She works long tyring hours. The only place she feels free and pieceful is at Blackbird Pond, where she can let go of her worries.

©1999 by Incentive Publications, Inc.
Nashville, TN.

Proofreading and Editing Activities for Writing

Book Report, Continued

One day Kit wanders into a meadow and meets Hannah, the Witch of Black bird Pond. When they're friendship is discovered kit is accused of whichcraft? Suddenly a mysterious fever spreads trhoughout the town. A few children die from this illness! Suspecting that she put an evil curse on the town. The angry people decide to burn Hannahs home.

I enjoyed this book. The characters thoughts and actions seemed especially beleiveable. Kit, my favorite character in the book, reminds me of several of my outspoken friends. Ms. Speare wrote this historical novel with excitement and zest. I highly recommend <u>The Witch of Blackbird Pond</u> because it is quite heartwarming and enlightening.

SPECIAL NOTE: There are over 30 corrections needed in the book report. Did you find all the errors? If not, reread the book report to see if you can find the errors you missed.

Name _____

©1999 by Incentive Publications, Inc.
Nashville, TN.

Proofreading and Editing Activities for Writing

Proofreading for Errors in an Outline

ACTIVITY: Carefully proofread the following outline for errors in the use of **Roman numerals, Arabic numerals,** and **capital letters.** Use the proofreading symbols (see page 5) to correct the errors. Copy the corrected outline on a separate sheet of paper.

Beginning a Coin collection

1.Reasons for Collecting Coins
    a. Pleasure
        1. Fun of watching collection grow
        2. appreciating variety of coins
    b. Educational Value
        I. Learning location of countries
        II. Learning about people and customs
II.Sources for the Collector
    A. loose change
    B. local bank
    c. hobby stores
    D. coin dealers
        1. Catalogs
        2. Proof sets
iii.Display for coins
    a. Supplies
        1. Collection Book
        2. Gloves
        3. plastic Sleeves
    b. Procedure
        1. checking coin
        2. Inserting coin
IV.Specialty For Coins

SPECIAL NOTE: There are 25 corrections needed in the outline. Did you find all the errors? If not, reread the outline to see if you can find the errors you missed.

Name _____

©1999 by Incentive Publications, Inc.
Nashville, TN.

Proofreading and Editing Activities for Writing

Additional Proofreading Symbols That Teachers Use

There are other proofreading symbols that teachers often use when correcting your paper. Here are some of the more commonly used proofreading symbols. You may notice that some of these symbols are different from those you have previously learned. When your teacher returns a paper to you, check here first for the meaning of the symbols.

SYMBOL	MEANING	CORRECTION
Cap	Begin word with a capital letter	Capitalize
lc	Lowercase	Use a small letter
frag	Sentence fragment	Make a whole sentence
r-o	Run-on sentence	Punctuate separately
gr	Mistake in grammar	Correct it
no ¶	No paragraph needed	Correct it
m?	Meaning unclear	Make it clear
s-v	Subject and verb do not agree	Make them agree
T	Mistake in verb tense	Correct the tense
K	Awkwardly expressed	Write it a better way
sp	Spelling mistake	Correct the spelling
rep	Repetition	Find another word
cut	Material is too long or too dull	Make it concise
dev	Develop	Add more detail
X	Obvious error	Correct it

Name _____

©1999 by Incentive Publications, Inc.
Nashville, TN.

Proofreading and Editing Activities for Writing

Proofreading Longer Selections for Errors

ACTIVITY: Proofread the following report "The Amish: Who Are They?" by Jonathan McCoy. Use the proofreading symbols (see page 5) to correct errors in **spelling, punctuation, capitalization, language usage, wordiness, transition,** and **clarity.** Copy the corrected report on a separate sheet of paper.

The Amish: Who Are They?
by Jonathan McCoy

The Amish have a different way of life than any other people around them. The Amish have always lived by their religious beliefs and followed the teachings of the Bible. The Amish aquired their name from Joseph Amman. Amman and his followers stressed a simple life. He stressed strict Church discipline. They believes in kicking out excommunicated members.

The Amish group in the seventeenth century origintated in Switzerland. William Penn invited them to the New World to settle in Pennsylvania. They welcomed the opportunity to escape religious persecution and go to a place in order to live in peace From 1710 to the end of the eighteenth century, the Amish settled along the streams and fertile valleys in Southeastern Pennsylvania. At present, the largest population of the Amish is located in Ohio. Throughout the United States, there are approximately 92,000 Amish.

Last summer my family and I visited an Amish community in Lancaster County, Pennsylvania. We toured a village where the homes were not like the homes of most Americans. In an Amish home they do not have electricity. In an Amish home there are no radios, televisions, or any other modern appliances. Coal, gas, or oil powered heaters are their only sources of heat. The Amish also have gas-powered refrigerators. Kerosene lamps or lamps are their main sources of light that burn naphtha. The Amish don't have no running water other than a small water pump that is used in the kitchen. Other sources of water must be pumped from an outdoor pump and carried into the house.

Meals are prepared and eaten in the kitchen, the largest and most commonly used room in the house. The kitchen is also used for playing games, reading, sewing, and doing schoolwork. All rooms, especaily the kitchen, are kept in spotless condition.

The Amish hold their worship services on Sunday. They are a very Christian group. Their services, sometimes held in members' homes or in a barn, begins at eight in the morning and last until noon. Men and Women are seated on wooden benches on different sides of the room. There worship services are usually attended by twenty-five to thirty families. The host family serves lunch to the congregation.

Name

Proofreading and Editing Activities for Writing

Proofreading Longer Selections for Errors, Continued

School is held in a one-room schoolhouse. The Amish children study spelling, penmanship, English, reading, and grammar. They also study arithmetic, social studies, and the Bible. Students attend school through the eighth grade from kintergarden. The Amish do not see a need for education beyond the eighth grade since they will be farming for a living. The school teacher is usually a young, un-married, Amish woman who has also only an eighth-grade education. She has been an apprentice in a classroom for two years. Amish children do not attend public schools. Because their parents do not want their children influenced by those not of their faith.

One way to identify an Amish person is by their dress. Most Amish clothing is homemade. Amish women are taught to sew at an early age. The women usually wear long, black, blue, or green dresses. Aprons are always worn over their dresses. If a woman is married the apron is black however, if she is unmarried, the apron is white. White caps are also worn. Jewelrey or colorful clothes are not allowed. Men dress in black or dark suits. Suspenders which do not have buttons or zippers are used to hold up their pants. Instead they have hook and eye fasteners. A black felt hat or straw hat completes their wardrobe. like their parents the Amish boys and girls dress. Men that are married must have beards but not mustaches.

Ownership of a farm is the primary goal of an Amish family. The Amish work hard on their farms. They take pride in them. Their farms are neat but not very large. Amish farm equipment has steel wheels and is powered by horses, mules, or both. If neighbors need equipment, he will lend it to them. The Amish crops usually consist of corn, barley, wheat, and a variety of vegetables. Tobaco is sometimes raised as a cash crop.

Amish funerals are rather standard. Both men and women are buried in white. After a person dies, he or she is buried three days later unless that day is a Sunday. The coffin is constructed of wood, The coffin is taken to the cemetary in a horse-drawn hearse. Because no flowers are laid on the grave the only marker is a tomb-stone. I found it interesting that the Amish believe in life after death, and their after-life is based on their earthly life.

Though my research, I have learned that the Amish people are deeply religious; they dress very simply; they do not use modern conveniences; and they are dedicated to farming. Although the outside world has been changing rapidly, the Amish only change and use new technology if it does not conflict with their basic beliefs.

SPECIAL NOTE: There are over 40 corrections needed in the report. Did you find all of the errors? If not, reread the report to see if you can find the errors you missed.

Name _____

©1999 by Incentive Publications, Inc.
Nashville, TN.

Proofreading and Editing Activities for Writing

Proofreading a Bibliography

ACTIVITY: Proofread the following bibliography *(a list of sources alphabetized by the last name of the author or the first word of the title).* Use the proofreading symbols (see page 5) to correct the errors in **form, spelling, punctuation,** and **capitalization.** Copy the corrected bibliography on a separate sheet of paper.

BIBLIOGROPHY

<u>Amish Country</u>. Gettysburg, Pennsylvania: TEM, Inc, 1988.

Bender, Harold S., and Smith, Henry C. "Mennonites and Their Herritage," <u>Mennonite Encyclopedia</u>. Scottdale, Pennsylvania: Good Books, 1964.

Davies, Blodwen. <u>String of Amber: The Heritage of the Mennonites</u>. Scottdale, Pennsylvania: Herald Press, 1973.

Denlinger, A. Martha. <u>real People</u>. Scottdale, Pennsylvania: Herald Press, 1986.

Hostetler John A. <u>Amish life</u>. Scottdale, Pennsylvania: Herald Press, 1983.

"Mennonites," Grolier Multimedia <u>Encyclopeadia</u>. CD-ROM. 1993.

Redekop, C.W. <u>Mennonite Society</u>. Scottdale, pennsylvania: Good Books, 1989.

Dyck, Cornelius J., ed. <u>Introduction to Mennonite History</u>. Scottdale, Pennsylvania: Herald Press, 1981

Scott, Stephen, and Pellman, Kenneth. Living Without Ellectricity. Scottdale, Pennsylvania: Good Books, 1990.

Williams, George H. <u>The Radical Reformation</u>. Gettysburg, Pennsylvania: Gettysburg Press, 1962.

SPECIAL NOTE: There are approximately 16 corrections needed in the bibliography. Did you find all of the errors? If not, reread the bibliography to see if you can find the errors you missed.

Name _____

©1999 by Incentive Publications, Inc.
Nashville, TN.

Chapter 7

Creative Writing and Proofreading for Success

In the final chapter, let's think of writing as fun . . . as one measure of success in your academic endeavors. Think of how exciting it would be to fill blank pages with words that make people laugh, wipe away tears, boil over with anger, stand up and cheer, or even race to the polls to vote. You will enjoy the satisfaction of creating sentences, paragraphs, stories, poems, letters, and even reports using your own words.

Have you ever thought of how many people write for a living or use some kind of writing in their everyday life? Professional writers include journalists, novelists, playwrights, poets, and script writers. Professional writers also include include people who teach others how to write. Doctors, lawyers, and teachers, as well as other business people, are often required to write articles as part of their profession. Writing advertisements for businesses, editing newspapers and magazines, creating instructional and technical manuals, and authoring textbooks all require proficient writers.

No one would expect someone who had only played baseball once in his life to be chosen to play for the Atlanta Braves. Nor would anyone expect a group who had never sung together to have a CD "go gold." So why would anyone expect good writing to occur without a great deal of practice and rewrites? An award-winning author must know the tools of good writing, including spelling, parts of speech, punctuation, capitalization, subject-verb agreement, transition, sentence variety, paragraphing, and clarity. It is the authors' hope that the exercises in this book will improve your proofreading and writing skills.

This chapter is designed to prepare you to be a better writer. As you work through the creative writing activities, keep in mind the old adage: *Practice makes perfect!* Finally, remember your successes as you write each activity.

Creative Writing and Proofreading for Success

Sentence Writing

ACTIVITY: Write at least one sentence about each of the following topics. Then exchange your paper with a classmate to proofread.

Write what you might say about . . .

1. your best friend's appearance . . . _____

   _____

   _____

2. your reaction to the food in the cafeteria . . . _____

   _____

   _____

3. directions to your house from school . . . _____

   _____

   _____

4. your favorite television personality . . . _____

   _____

   _____

5. the last time you visited the zoo . . . _____

   _____

   _____

6. your favorite school field trip last year . . . _____

   _____

   _____

7. your memory of your first-grade teacher . . . _____

   _____

   _____

8. the day your family bought a pet . . . _____

   _____

   _____

Name _____

©1999 by Incentive Publications, Inc.
Nashville, TN.

Creative Writing and Proofreading for Success

Writing Descriptive Paragraphs

One might define a **paragraph** as the development of one main idea or topic. The **topic sentence** (usually the first or second sentence) indicates what this main idea will be. When the reader knows the topic, then he or she is able to follow the writer's idea easily. The remainder of the paragraph consists of sentences that explain or develop the main idea. Paragraphs furnish a way for a writer to establish his or her thoughts. Each new paragraph should be a signal that the writer is about to develop a new idea or change direction in some way. Paragraphs also help readers keep track of the author's various points without becoming confused.

When you describe someone or something, you draw a picture of it with your words. A **descriptive paragraph,** then, is a paragraph that describes something. The purpose of a description is to make the reader see, hear, or experience something. The best way to make a reader feel that what you are describing is real is to appeal to the senses. Try to be as specific as possible; however, like a good narrative, a good description omits unnecessary details.

ACTIVITY: Search your memory for an event, a place, or a person that you could describe in a descriptive paragraph, or choose one of the topics listed below. Write a descriptive paragraph of approximately 100 words on a separate sheet of paper. Be sure to include a topic sentence. Ask a classmate to proofread your finished paragraph for errors.

1. A most impressive summer at the Grand Canyon

2. Riding home on the school bus

3. My memories of the best amusement park

4. The street near my house after school

5. The best baseball game ever

6. One of the most interesting characters

7. The school cafeteria during the lunch hour

8. Our classroom during a test

9. The park near my home

10. My most memorable parade

Name _____

©1999 by INCENTIVE PUBLICATIONS, Inc.
Nashville, TN.

Creative Writing and Proofreading for Success

Creating "Inflationary Words"

THE RISING COST OF LANGUAGE

Inflation is a growing concern to all of us. Prices keep rising higher and higher. Almost everything is worth more today than it was yesterday; therefore, our language needs adjusting.

Shouldn't *tennis* be *elevennis? Go forth* should become *go fifth.* And *Mary Tyler Moore* should really be *Mary Tyler Much Moore. Before* could become *befive,* and even *tulips* would inflate to *threelips.*

Think of as many words as you can with numbers in them or **homonyms** of number words. Rewrite them, raising each one number. For example, *Officiate = Officinine; Don Juan = Don Two;* and *Canine = Caten.*

ACTIVITY: Here's a great chance for you to be creative. Use the inflationary words you listed from the above exercise to develop your own *inflationary dictionary;* to write an *inflationary letter;* or to create an *inflationary story.*

Five score and eight years ago our fivefathers set fifth. OR Twice upon a time . . .

_____

_____

_____

_____

_____

_____

_____

_____

_____

_____

_____

_____

_____

Name _____

Creative Writing and Proofreading for Success

Writing A Letter of Invitation

ACTIVITY: You have just run out of holiday party invitations; however, you have one more friend to invite. Write a letter inviting your friend to your holiday party. Be sure to include all the important information from your party invitation.

After writing the letter, proofread it for errors in spelling, capitalization, and punctuation.

_____
(your street address)

_____
(your city, state, and ZIP)

_____
(today's date)

_____,

_____

_____

_____

_____

_____

_____

_____

_____

_____

_____

_____

Name _____

Creative Writing and Proofreading for Success

Cartoons for Creative Writing

    Cartoons have always had a universal appeal. Everyone of practically every age enjoys reading cartoons. The two cartoons pictured below have been created to encourage you to write. Study each of these cartoons. Then write a short reaction to each on a separate sheet of paper. Before you write your response, think about the answers to the questions listed.

Cartoon Response

    When Mullen's Shoes has a sale, "Buy One Pair, Get the Second Pair Half Price" is frequently used. Why do you think shoe stores use this sales offer? Will customers take advantage of this sale? Would you want to take advantage of this offer? Could you offer any advice to the shoe store owner?

Cartoon Response

    What do you think the waitress has just asked the diner? Why do you think the man is so puzzled? What type of dinner do you think he has selected? What do you think of the waitress? Do you think the man will enjoy this meal? What advice would you give the diner?

Name _____

©1999 by Incentive Publications, Inc.
Nashville, TN.

Creative Writing and Proofreading for Success

Book Report Mobile*

After you have read a book, recall the beginning, middle, and ending highlights. Select memorable events from each section that will accurately depict the scenes and plot from your book. Prepare illustrations and brief summaries for each highlighted section. As you prepare your summaries, check for spelling, capitalization, punctuation, and organization.

These items can be creatively displayed in a mobile format. The materials needed for this activity are as follows:
- Wire coat hanger
- String
- Construction paper
- Markers
- Pen
- Glue
- Scissors

Prepare each illustration and summary on construction paper two times. Cut these out and glue them back-to-back with a string inserted through each illustration and summary. Tie the strings on the hanger. Place the beginning illustration and summary on the left and continue tying the other items from left to right in the order of the events in the book.

Give a "book talk" to your classmates by telling the class about your mobile. Display your mobile in your classroom or in the media center.

*Used with permission from Jennifer Moore, Teacher, Sara Smith School, Atlanta Public Schools, Atlanta, Georgia.

Name _____

Creative Writing and Proofreading for Success

Billboard Advertising

Billboard advertising is perhaps one of the most popular forms of advertising. We all have seen the big billboards with large pictures and flashing lights along the highways as well as in the cities.

In this activity you will create an ad for a large billboard that thousands will see as they travel by it each day. Be sure to proofread for errors in spelling, capitalization, punctuation, and usage.

ACTIVITY: First, choose a company that sells a product that you really like or enjoy. You might choose a company that sells food products or a company that is in the fashion industry. Next, decide how you would promote the product. Decide on the graphics or photograph to be used on the billboard. Now create a slogan to promote your product. Write your description of the billboard and your slogan on the lines provided.

Name of company and product: _____

_____

Description of graphics or photograph that will be used on the billboard:

_____

_____

_____

_____

_____

_____

_____

_____

Billboard slogan:_____

_____

_____

Name _____

Creative Writing and Proofreading for Success

Writing a Group Poem

    Most poems are written by individual authors; however, during this activity, you will work with four or five other students to create a group poem. Every student in the group will write at least one line of the poem; then, he or she will pass the paper to the next person. The next writer will then read as well as proofread what the first writer has written and add at least one other line to the poem. The paper then passes to the next writer in the group, and so on. It is extremely important that the poem stay with the same subject and style selected by the first person. Remember, if the first lines of the poem rhyme, then the additional lines must also rhyme. The last person who receives the poem must not only write the lines that complete the poem but must also proofread the entire poem for any errors. Finally, the poem is returned to the writer of the first lines. The "first writer" must now edit the entire poem and write a final copy.

Title of Poem: _____

_____

_____

_____

_____

_____

_____

_____

_____

_____

_____

_____

_____

_____

_____

_____

_____

Name _____

©1999 by Incentive Publications, Inc.
Nashville, TN.

Creative Writing and Proofreading for Success

Writing a Short Story

ACTIVITY: Everyone enjoys reading a great short story. There are many topics you can explore. Here are just a few suggestions:

- Write a story telling what you like or dislike about school.
- Write a story describing a fictitious person, and make the reader like or dislike this person from your description.
- Write a story in which you leave an important message for future generations.
- Write a story in which you woke up one morning and found that there was nobody else in your house, city, or even in the whole country.

When you finish your short story, ask a classmate to proofread it for any errors.

A Short Story

by _____

_____

_____

_____

_____

_____

_____

_____

_____

_____

_____

_____

_____

_____

(Use additional paper to complete your short story.)

Name _____

©1999 by Incentive Publications, Inc.
Nashville, TN.

Proofreader's

Certificate

This is to certify that

_____
(Name)

has been awarded this certificate of proofreading excellence and has demonstrated the ability to recognize errors in spelling, capitalization, punctuation, and usage. The recipient has also demonstrated competence in creative writing.

_____
(School)

_____
(Teacher's Signature)

_____
(Date)

Chapter 1

6

Building Proofreading Skills in Spelling

Spelling mistakes can prevent others from seeing your great ideas in print. This chapter will help you learn to avoid common spelling errors through a variety of carefully selected activities. Many spelling mistakes come from careless haste. Whenever you write, proofread your paper not only for difficult words, but also for simple, ordinary words that you may have misspelled through carelessness.

How to Improve Your Spelling of Particular Words:
1. Find out what your personal spelling demons are and conquer them.
2. Keep a good dictionary nearby to use whenever in doubt.
3. Pronounce words correctly; this will help you write them correctly.
4. Get into the habit of taking a good look at new or difficult words.
5. Develop your own memory device (called a **mnemonic**) for difficult words.

PRETEST: Each item below gives four possible spellings of a word. Read the words, and circle the letter of the correct spelling.

Sample:
a. apoligize	(b.) apologize	c. eplogize	d. epoligize

1. a. formela | b. fourmula | (c.) formula | d. foremulla
2. (a.) concession | b. concesion | c. consetion | d. consession
3. a. gratfull | (b.) grateful | c. greatful | d. gradeful
4. a. annoience | b. annoiance | c. anoyence | (d.) annoyance
5. (a.) hastily | b. hastilie | c. hastely | d. hastyly
6. a. triplacate | b. tripleacate | (c.) triplicate | d. triplicte
7. a. justefid | (b.) justified | c. justifyed | d. justifeyed
8. a. stabillaty | b. stabbility | c. stabilaty | (d.) stability

7

Building Proofreading Skills in Spelling

ie and ei Spelling Errors

Rule 1: Write *ie* when the sound is *long e* (grief, believe, relief), except after c (deceive, receive, conceive). **Exceptions:** *neither, leisure, seize*

Rule 2: Write *ei* when the sound is not *long e*, especially when the sound is *long a* (sleigh, foreign, freight). **Exceptions:** *friend, mischief, soldier*

ACTIVITY: Proofread the following paragraph. Add either *ie* or *ei* to complete the words.

Sample:

The for**ei**gn sold**ie**r accidentally dropped his sh**ie**ld in the f**ie**ld.

Recently our n**ei**ghborhood held its annual picnic in the baseball f**ie**ld near the ch**ie**f of police's house. We ate lots of food—w**ie**ners, corn on the cob, and p**ie**ces of cake. Some of the people started playing w**ei**rd games, combining softball and soccer. While we were playing ball, the misch**ie**vous children said they saw a th**ie**f race through the picnic area and rel**ie**ve us of all the sandwiches. My n**ie**ce did not bel**ie**ve them, so she began to give the children gr**ie**f. One of her fr**ie**nds said that he saw the real th**ie**ves.

Suddenly, the smiling children returned the sandwiches, and we enjoyed the rest of our l**ei**sure time. At the end of the afternoon, our grandfather presented special ach**ie**vement awards to all except the "misch**ie**vous" children.

8

Building Proofreading Skills in Spelling

-able and -ible Spelling Errors

Because the *-able* and *-ible* endings usually sound the same, sound is not a good clue to use when deciding which spelling to use. A good general rule to remember is that *-able* occurs more often as a suffix than *-ible*.

Rule 1: If the word ends in a consonant followed by an *e*, the *e* is dropped before adding *-ible* or *-able*. **Exceptions:** words ending in *ce* or *ge*, such as *noticeable* and *knowledgeable*.

Rule 2: If a word ends in *y*, add the suffix *-able*, not *-ible*. The *y* will change to *i* as in *reliable*, or it will drop as in *charitable*.

ACTIVITY: Each item below lists four possible spellings of a word. Read the words, and circle the letter of the correct spelling.

Sample:
a. charartible	(b.) charitable	c. charatable	d. charitible

1. a. iratible | (b.) irritable | c. iritable | d. irratable
2. a. relieable | b. relible | c. relyable | (d.) reliable
3. (a.) reducible | b. reducable | c. reduceable | d. reduceible
4. a. legable | b. leggible | (c.) legible | d. leggable
5. a. comvertable | b. convirtible | c. convertable | (d.) convertible
6. a. misrible | (b.) miserable | c. misrable | d. misarible
7. (a.) respectable | b. respectible | c. respecable | d. respecible
8. a. incredable | b. increable | (c.) incredible | d. increible
9. a. imaginible | b. imagenable | (c.) imaginable | d. immaginable
10. (a.) indisputable | b. indesputible | c. innisputable | d. indisputible

9

Building Proofreading Skills in Spelling

-ant, -ent, -ance, and -ence Spelling Errors

In words with the *-ant, -ent, -ance,* or *-ence* endings, sound is not a very good clue to the spelling of the endings. There is, however, a good way to remember whether a word is spelled with *-ant* or *-ent*, or whether it is spelled with *-ance* or *-ence*. Look at the following word pairs:

assist**ant**—assist**ance**   intellig**ent**—intellig**ence**

The words in each pair are related in meaning and in spelling. So, if you are uncertain about whether the spelling of an ending is *-ant* or *-ent*, or *-ance* or *-ence*, think of the related word.

ACTIVITY: Proofread the following paragraph, using *-ant, -ent, -ance,* or *-ence* to complete the words. Write the correct letters in each blank.

Sample:
The opening number in the award-winning musical was quite magnific**ent**.

When our test scores were returned last week, Mr. Thomas announced that we had made signific**ant** improvement. He was pleased with our overall, brilli**ant** scores. For the first time ever, Mr. Thomas filled our class with unbelievable confid**ence**. He also attributed part of the results to our outstanding attend**ance** record.

Louise remarked, "Mr. Thomas, we all feel that your pati**ence** has contributed a great deal to our ability to learn this year."

Another student stated gleefully, "Without your assist**ance** in algebra, we would not feel as confid**ent**."

"Students," Mr. Thomas replied, "your intellig**ence** has been there all along. I'm just so glad that I could help all of you realize your true, magnific**ent** ability."

BONUS:
Write a few sentences or a short paragraph using words ending with *-ant, -ent, -ance,* and *-ence.* Spell some of the words correctly and some incorrectly. Then, exchange papers with a classmate to proofread.

Building Proofreading Skills in Spelling
-ary, -ery, and -ory Spelling Errors

Sometimes the sound of the ending is a good clue to its spelling, as in dormit*ory* and ordin*ary*. In many words, however, the vowel sounds are unaccented, and thus the sound is not a good clue to its spelling, as in batt*ery* and summ*ary*. **Hint:** Most of the time adjectives use the *-ary* ending, as in revolution*ary*, and nouns use the *-ery* ending, as in scen*ery*.

An Unusual Tour

Calinda and her sister Frieda arrived at the cemet*ery* at 2 P.M. The tour of the city would begin there. The scen*ery* was beautiful, although the tempor*ary* shelter that had been erected at the site was very ordin*ary*.

Calinda wondered what kind of sal*ary* the tour guides earn. Their tour guide seemed to have an extraordin*ary* amount of knowledge about the hist*ory* of the city. The guide began telling Frieda and Calinda about the myst*ery* concerning one of the graves.

Apparently during the time of the Revolution*ary* War, a man was accused of creating a forg*ery* of a document. The man was believed to have been caught, killed, and buried in the cemet*ery*. However, when the grave was excavated much later, no body was found in the coffin.

After listening to the mysterious tale, the two sisters then toured the laborat*ory* of a well-known scientist. Later, they visited a building that was used as a dormit*ory* for a private school. The girls thoroughly enjoyed their visit. They vowed to return even as they passed the bound*ary* of the old city and set out toward home.

Building Proofreading Skills in Spelling
Spelling Homonyms Correctly

Below is a list of commonly used **homonyms** (words that sound the same, but have different spellings and meanings) of which proofreaders need to be aware.

their	to	rain
there	too	reign
they're	two	rein
coarse	threw	pear
course	through	pair
stationary	capital	who's
stationery	capitol	whose
principal	your	
principle	you're	

ACTIVITY: Proofread the sentences below. Correct the misused homonyms, using the proofreading symbols, (see page 5) to insert or delete letters as needed. *Hint:* When choosing a homonym, always think about what the word *means* in the sentence.

Sample: Who's reference books are these on the table in the library?

1. The principle corrected the students in the hallway by repeating one of the golden principals.
2. Will you please pass the peal of gloves lying near the jar of pairs on the table.
3. Jill wrote her letter on the new lavender stationary since she had to remain stationery in her room for the afternoon.
4. To many children are going two several events during the too days of the festival.
5. There are often too many students going to *their* (they're) lockers when there supposed to be in there classes.
6. Remember to use a capital letter when spelling Washington, D.C., our nation's capital.
7. For *your* science test, your required to learn the parts of a flower.

Building Proofreading Skills in Spelling
Spelling

ACTIVITY: Each item below gives three possible spellings of a word. Read the words, and circle the correct spelling.

Sample:

trater	triater	(traitor)
1. athelete	athalete	(athlete)
2. (library)	libeary	libary
3. (February)	Febuary	Febrary
4. govenor	govener	(governor)
5. angal	(angle)	angol
6. arthur	(author)	althur
7. (sincerely)	sinserely	sincerly
8. rythm	(rhythm)	rhithm
9. (unusual)	unusal	unusuall
10. musel	mussul	(muscle)
11. tomatos	tomatoess	(tomatoes)
12. photoe	foto	(photo)
13. (separate)	seperate	sepparate
14. pressence	(presence)	prescence
15. omited	(omitted)	ommitted
16. aukward	awkword	(awkward)

BONUS:
Make a list of ten words that you misspell often, spelling them incorrectly. Then give the list to a classmate to proofread and correct.

Building Proofreading Skills in Spelling
Spelling

ACTIVITY: Proofread the following phrases. In most of the phrases, there will be one misspelled word. Underline the misspelled word and, in the blank provided, write the word correctly. If there are no misspelled words, write *none* in the blank.

Sample

at the new Olympic Stadium in Atlanta — *none*

1. must tell people of your true <u>fellings</u> — *feelings*
2. think carefully about your own <u>writing</u> — *writing*
3. the unusual statement of <u>porpose</u> — *purpose*
4. <u>refusse</u> to be closely involved — *refuse*
5. to discover her own natural ability — *none*
6. enables the large, beautiful bird to fly — *none*
7. his unbiased political <u>opinon</u> of the candidate — *opinion*
8. due north of <u>metropolitin</u> Chicago — *metropolitan*
9. to talk Carlos out of <u>atending</u> the football game — *attending*
10. the old <u>ferosious</u> lion in the zoo — *ferocious*
11. destined to win the state championship title — *none*
12. seemed totally <u>asttonished</u> about the murder — *astonished*
13. <u>intervue</u> the anxious applicant at the office — *interview*
14. tall, muscular, intense <u>marshell</u> at the jail — *marshal*
15. caught a quick <u>glimse</u> of the movie star — *glimpse*

©1999 by Incentive Publications, Inc.
Nashville, TN.

14

Building Proofreading Skills in Spelling
Spelling

ACTIVITY: Proofread each sentence carefully and circle the misspelled words. Then write the correct spelling on the blanks provided. You may not need all of the blanks.

Sample:

At the delicatessen they served delicious ham sandwiches.   *delicatessen*

1. The Atlanta Braves' uniforms have a red tomahwak on the front.   *tomahawk*

2. On this particuler evening, we went to the nearby restaurant to eat steak and potatoes.   *particular*

3. The old woman beleived that the pathetic begger was truly in desperate need.   *believed* *beggar*

4. The county ambulence raced quickly to the tragic scene of the traffic accidant.   *ambulance* *accident*

5. One rhinoceros was slautered for his valuable horn.   *slaughtered*

6. When the two old friends met, they sat and began to reminise about their childhood.   *reminisce*

7. The magnifisence of the sunset was indescribable.   *magnificence*

8. The temperature in the Artic was extremely friggid all year long.   *Arctic* *frigid*

9. I wonder if that animal I saw in the woods was a racoon or an opossum.   *raccoon*

10. Is a canteloup considered a vegatable or a fruit?   *Cantaloupe* *vegetable*

11. The clever thieves were thorogh when they robbed the house.   *thieves* *thorough*

12. Ashley and her freind finaly decided to go to the movies.   *friend* *finally*

15

Building Proofreading Skills in Spelling
Spelling

ACTIVITY: Proofread the following paragraphs for spelling errors. Circle the misspelled words and then, on the line provided, write the correct spelling of each word.

Sample:

The wonerful employees at Della's Gift Shop were treated to a dinner party honering all employees who had served over five years.   *wonderful* *honoring*

Snakes

Snakes are in the reptile family and are closely related to lizards. They are covered with numberous small scales, which are overlapping. They have moveable eyelids and external ear openings. They use their tongues to smell. The smallest snake is 8–12 inches long and the largest measures about 8 feet.   *reptile* *numerous* *movable* *tongues* *measures*

Snakes are carnivores, which means they are meat-eaters. They find their pray by smell and sight, but they don't see well. They eat their prey whole. Some snakes kill by constrition, some by prompt swalowing and others kill by poisoning. Their jaws aren't atachhed and this helps them swallow their food. Their teeth also aid them in eatting. Many snakes eat rats and mice, and it may take 4–6 days to digest a meal. Some snakes are beleived to be able to go two years without food.   *carnivores* *prey* *constriction* *swallowing* *attached* *eating* *believed*

From: *Effective Language Arts Techniques for Middle Grades*, by Brenda Opie and Douglas McAvinn, Incentive Publications, Nashville, Tennessee, 1995.

16

Building Proofreading Skills in Spelling
Spelling

ACTIVITY: Here's a real challenge in proofreading for spelling errors! First, look at the list of words below and circle the correct spelling of each word. Next, read the sentences and, in the blank provided, write the correct spelling of the word that best completes each sentence.

proceed	OR	prosede
recieved	OR	received
circuit	OR	sircuit
exceed	OR	exsede
voloenteered	OR	volunteered
prospector	OR	prospecter
sucede	OR	succeed
miserible	OR	miserable
patience	OR	patience
divisible	OR	divisable
excelerate	OR	accelerate

Sample:

The car began to _accelerate_ rapidly down the road.

1. The electric _circuit_ was overloaded and caused a fire.

2. How will the meeting _proceed_ without our chairperson?

3. Munga wanted to _succeed_ Maria as Henderson student council president.

4. The police officer warned us not to _exceed_ the speed limit in her town.

5. Please demonstrate your _patience_ while waiting for your appointment.

6. Is the number 56 _divisible_ by 8 or 6?

7. Natasha was certainly _miserable_ after her appendectomy.

8. Umar, our exchange student from Saudi Arabia, _volunteered_ to help us.

9. The _prospector_ went into the Rockies and struck gold immediately.

10. When I attended the Garth Brooks concert, he _received_ a standing ovation.

17

Building Proofreading Skills in Spelling
Spelling

ACTIVITY: Proofread the following paragraphs for spelling errors. Circle all the misspelled words. Then, write the correct spelling of each misspelled word on the line provided.

Sample:

Antartica the coolest place on earth, is the fifth largest continent. This ice-covered area completly encircles the South Pole.   *Antarctica* *completely*

VACATION AT MULBERRY POND
(JOURNAL: JUNE 20, 19___)

Colors of mostly orange and yellow began to drifft in the sky as a welcomming sunrise fell upon Mulberry in the warm morning that I arrived. Rays of gold danced on the pond, beckkening me to the water to soothe the summer heat. Haridly waiting for the car to come to a standstill, I mediattely dashed for the pond, with renewed memories of last summer and what lay in store for me this summer.   *drift* *welcoming* *beckoning* *Hardly* *immediately*

Retreeting to this secluded log cabin out in the middle of the forest has been our family tradtion for years. The pond reaches out into the pine trees, giving beauty to the surounding wilderness. Accustomed to friendly human life, animals rome the area with the same kind of contentmnt that the pond seems to reflect. And the lush green grass around the pond wilingly supports all kinds of ladybugs and butterflies.   *Retreating* *tradition* *surrounding* *roam* *contentment* *willingly*

From: *Preparing Students to Raise Achievement Scores* [Grades 5–6], Incentive Publications, Inc., Nashville, Tennessee, 1996.

Building Proofreading Skills

Building Proofreading Skills in Capitalization

Because it is important to learn how to communicate with written language, proper capitalization is essential. The purpose of this chapter is to develop and improve your capitalization skills in proofreading. Remember, proper nouns, pronouns, and proper adjectives are capitalized, and the first word in every sentence is capitalized. Working through these carefully selected exercises will improve your writing skills as well as your capitalization and proofreading skills.

PRETEST: Proofread each sentence carefully. Use the proofreading symbol for capitalization (see page 5), to correct each word that should be capitalized.

Sample:

We enjoyed french bread with our meal.

1. Were you born in december?
2. I met prince Charles in london.
3. Sue enjoyed reading *little women*.
4. it happened the last day of january.
5. what is the population of china now?
6. Tom said, "i need a new skateboard."
7. halloween, my favorite holiday, is in october.
8. Our class visited rabbi rosenbaum.
9. my favorite book is sounder.
10. carrie's mother bought a new mustang.
11. mail the letter to mayor campbell.
12. Our school has many spanish students.
13. Our family went to florida for vacation.
14. My brother attends columbia university.
15. We crossed the golden gate bridge.
16. My sister joined the girl scouts.
17. please finish your reports by thursday.
18. We thought uncle walter had arrived.

Building Proofreading Skills in Capitalization
Capitalization

ACTIVITY: Read the following list of words. In each line there is one word that does not require a capital letter. On the blank provided, write the word that does not require any capitalization.

> **Rule 1:** Capitalize proper nouns and proper adjectives (*July, Buddhist*).
> **Rule 2:** Capitalize geographical names (*Haiti, Atlantic Ocean*).
> **Rule 3:** Capitalize a person's title only if followed by their name (*doctor, Doctor Smith*).
> **Rule 4:** Capitalize the pronoun *I*.

Sample:

	Melinda	February	Senator	Bolivia	*senator*
1.	Joseph	Laos	Doctor	England	*doctor*
2.	France	Mister	Melinda	Congress	*mister*
3.	President	Elizabeth	Ed	Donald	*president*
4.	Dallas	Aunt	America	Halloween	*aunt*
5.	Mother	Sunday	Ohio	Ontario	*mother*
6.	Swedish	Europe	Queen	Georgia	*queen*
7.	I'm	Isn't	I'd	I'll	*isn't*
8.	Billy	Spanish	Asia	Actor	*actor*
9.	Paris	Avenue	Peru	California	*avenue*
10.	Burma	Martha	Spain	Island	*island*
11.	Liberty	Russian	Jonathan	June	*liberty*
12.	Harriett	Roger	Desert	Mississippi	*desert*
13.	Patricia	City	Blanca	Patrick	*city*
14.	August	Thursday	Caesar	Street	*street*
15.	Easter	Africa	Winter	Beverly	*winter*

Building Proofreading Skills in Capitalization
Capitalization

ACTIVITY: Using all of the previously stated rules of capitalization, proofread the following phrases for errors. Use the proofreading symbols for capitalization (see page 5) to mark the word(s) that should be capitalized. Hint: Some phrases do not contain any errors in capitalization. If there are no mistakes in the phrase, write none to the left of the phrase.

Sample:

the postcard I sent to jim

none 1. one of our police officers
2. president Wilson of the United States
3. just the other day my dad and bob
4. aunt rose, one of my favorite aunts,
5. here at Westlake mall we always
6. billy, my brother's nickname,
7. to his favorite doctor, doctor cook,
8. the number of the new house on oak street
none 9. into the cold water of the lake
10. always wanted to live as a southeasterner
11. to lake superior after their wedding
12. roads like Beverly Hills' rodeo drive
13. a 1965 ford mustang in perfect condition
none 14. driving to the southeast side of the city
15. at sutton middle school in Atlanta, Georgia

BONUS:

Write a short paragraph about one of your heroes. Include several errors in capitalization. Exchange papers with one of your classmates to proofread.

Building Proofreading Skills in Capitalization
Capitalization

ACTIVITY: Using all of the rules of capitalization, proofread the following sentences for errors. Use the proofreading symbols for capitalization (see page 5) to mark the word(s) that should be capitalized and those that should be lowercase.

Sample:

The new Student, Jason Richards, is originally from toledo, ohio.

1. When we were in Wyoming last Summer, We visited yellowstone national Park.
2. when we last saw Sheri, she was driving West on McDonough street.
3. The tara theater is located near the Hotel on Cheshire Bridge road.
4. one of the most breathtaking bridges in the world is the golden gate bridge.
5. My Grandmother visited the smoky mountains where thousands of cherokee Indians live.
6. In just a few minutes, the president of the United States will address congress.
7. Norway, Sweden, denmark, and Finland make up the scandinavian Countries.
8. While my Father was waiting to interview the Mayor, he read the *miami Herald*.
9. When school begins, I will be taking English, spanish, world History, and science.
10. Alex Haley, the author of *roots*, traced the History of his own family.
11. Many of the Cereal Companies have lowered their prices.
12. one of my favorite television shows is *friends*, which airs every thursday Night.
13. During the spring holidays, we visited Disneyworld and toured universal studios.
14. The reverend William McKoy introduced the renowned speaker, dr. wai phing choo.
15. Please mail your reply to 4536 North Druid hills road, atlanta, GA 30329.
16. Edgar has been a Member of the young men's Christian Association for 12 years.
17. let's ask bishop Wendell to give the commencement address.
18. One of my favorite books from last year's readings was *animal farm*.
19. If you want to get to Shady Valley Park, go North on Lenox road.

©1999 by Incentive Publications, Inc.
Nashville, TN.

Building Proofreading Skills in Capitalization
Capitalization

22

ACTIVITY: Proofread the following phrases. Use the proofreading symbol for lowercase (see page 5) to mark the word(s) that should NOT be capitalized. *Hint:* Some phrases do not contain any mistakes in capitalization.

    Rule 1: Capitalize the first word in a sentence, not in a phrase.
    Rule 2: Capitalize the main words in the name of an important document.
    Rule 3: Capitalize the names of ships, planets, monuments, awards, and any particular places, parks, things, or historical events.
    Rule 4: Capitalize the names of nationalities, races, and religions.
    Rule 5: Do not capitalize the names of school subjects, except languages and course names followed by a number.

Sample:
    the favorite Poet of all time

1. every year my Family travels through
2. chose a seat on the East side
3. while writing the Declaration of Independence
4. climbed the Highest Mountain in the world
5. Elizabeth, the Queen of England
6. days when my Brother and I spend time together
7. ate Swedish Pancakes for breakfast
8. the Chinese Manager of Yung's new company
9. the last name of the Princess of Monaco
10. my favorite part of the Country
11. watched the Pilot land the Plane on the runway
12. took a tour of the Museum
13. the Fourth Thursday in November
14. in the Beautiful Spring weather
15. an African-American woman we studied in History
16. on the Ship the *S.S. Queen Elizabeth*

Building Proofreading Skills in Capitalization
Capitalization

23

ACTIVITY: Proofread the following sentences for errors in capitalization. Using the proofreading symbols for lowercase and capitalization (see page 5), mark those word(s) that should be capitalized and those that should NOT be capitalized.

    Rule 1: The first word of a sentence that is a direct quotation is capitalized even if the quotation begins within another sentence (*Marcie shouted, "She did it!"*)
    Rule 2: Capitalize the first word and all important words in titles of magazines, books, newspapers, poems, stories, movies, and works of art (*Roots*).
    Rule 3: Capitalize names of organizations, business firms, institutions, and government bodies (*Future Teachers of America*).

Sample:
    my aunt Sandy from salt lake City is a good Mother to all of her children.

1. "oh no," said mother, " i never told john that he could go to the concert."
2. How does the Doctor feel about the Treatment of his Cancer?
3. Poonam and her Sister have gone to the Store to buy some vegetables and fruit.
4. On Jekyll Island, off the coast of georgia, there is a 4-h facility.
5. King Ferdinand and his Queen did not want to give the Explorer any money.
6. How did the governor of california manage to accomplish all of his Goals?
7. in the state of south dakota, you will find mount rushmore.
8. The Book, *The Red pony*, by John Steinbeck is set during the Great depression.
9. roberto likes to watch the latin american dancers in their beautiful costumes.
10. Inga enjoys reading the national geographic magazine.
11. *The pet detective*, starring Jim Carey, is perhaps my favorite Movie.
12. Gandhi spoke spanish, german, and french as well as his native language, hindi.
13. "Where The Sidewalk Ends" by shel silverstein is one of my favorite Poems.
14. Did you know that kwanzaa is celebrated in december by many african-Americans?
15. In mexico my friends celebrate cinco de mayo in the Spring.

Building Proofreading Skills in Capitalization
Capitalization

24

ACTIVITY: Using all of the previously stated rules of capitalization, proofread the following phrases for errors. Use the proofreading symbols for lowercase and capitalization (see page 5) to mark the word(s) that should be capitalized as well as those that should NOT be capitalized.

Sample:
    the Part of niagara falls in the United States

1. to get to my house from oakland city Schools
2. an odd Area of the atlantic ocean
3. a winding River bordering illinois and iowa
4. the Battlefield at Gettysburg, pennsylvania
5. the atacama desert in the South American Country of chile
6. six blocks South of North Druid Hills road
7. a well-known eastern University in Massachusetts
8. the biggest Football Game of the year
9. in 1492 christopher columbus and his Crew
10. in the Movie, *the Shawshank redemption*
11. My Short Story, "The King Of The court"
12. in the *New York Times* Article on sunday
13. athens, the Home of the University Of georgia
14. north of the caribbean Island of puerto rico
15. is celebrated with Parades in New York city
16. during the great depression of the 1930s
17. boarded the amtrak train in Carlsbad, New mexico
18. To open our Textbooks to Chapter 10 Today

Building Proofreading Skills in Capitalization
Capitalization

25

ACTIVITY: From the following students' original paragraphs, correct any errors in capitalization by using the proofreading symbols (see page 5).

My Basketball Hero
by Bob Wechsler

    I simply love the game of Basketball, and I chose Anfernee "penny" Hardaway as my Basketball Hero. He plays for the orlando Magic. The reasons i chose him are his Attitude and focus on his Goals. Whether it is on or Off the Basketball Court, "penny" stays focused. I would like to be as focused on my Personal goals and be as successful as Hardaway.

Martin Luther King, Jr., My Hero
by Alexandra Lentz

    i consider dr. Martin Luther King, jr., to be a Hero because he was determined and dedicated to his work. dr. King was a good leader and wanted to help other people. He fought for the Freedom of African-americans, and now his Dream has come true. He was so determined that people finally changed the Laws. He also gave people Ideas to think about.

My Mother, My Hero
by Kermit Finch

    Mrs. ellen Finch, my Mother, is also my hero. Her ability to understand me is her Strength. Responsibility is a big part of her Life. No matter what the circumstances, She always gets the job done. i praise her for her reminders. I probably would have failed at least one class (english) if she had not helped me with my homework. She is strict, never letting Anyone get the best of her, but she always has room for fun.

Building Proofreading Skills in Capitalization
Capitalization

ACTIVITY: Use the proofreading symbols (see page 5) to correct the errors in capitalization from Brandon Barnett's "Space Exploration" paper.

Space Exploration
by Brandon Barnett

The u.s. and many other countries plan to start colonizing space. This project will be an international effort. Plans for an international space station are in the making. this project will be used to help the world control its population problem.

n.a.s.a. has already made plans to start building an international space station by the year 2000. The parts will be ferried up by the space shuttle over a period of several missions. Millions of dollars will be spent for the astronauts to accomplish this job.

If this project is a success, people will start moving to self-contained colonies. The countries of england, france, and the united states have already started pouring dollars into this project.

colonizing planets will give people the chance to explore new frontiers. At one time this was only a dream, but in the future it will become a reality.

BONUS:
Write a paragraph about a historic place that you have visited or would like to visit. Include errors in capitalization. Give the unedited paragraph to a classmate to proofread.

Building Proofreading Skills in Capitalization
Cumulative Review
Spelling and Capitalization

ACTIVITY: Use the proofreading symbols (see page 5) to correct the errors in spelling and capitalization from Rachel Gottschalk's paper "The Scariest Night of My Life."

The Scariest Night of My Life
by Rachel Gottschalk

October 31, 1995, i was going trick-or-treatin with some of my friends. I put on my costume and found my bag, just like any other halloween night. Little did i know this would be the scariest night of my life (so far)!

we went the usual route (around my neighborhood), down Henderson mill road. When we were finished, it was only 8:00 P.M. My friends and i decided to try a new path. We went through glen rose street. By the time we were finished, our bags were full, and we were geting bored.

then one of my friends said, "you know that old Henderson cemetary near here? let's go there."

We all looked at each other, and everyone agreed we should go. I was a little scared, but I couldn't chicken out now.

The cemetary was so old that the stones had eroded and some of the graves had caved in. The lights were on in the nearby houses, so it was not too scarry. We were walking quietly through, when I sliped into one of the old graves! (it may not seem scarry to you, but it scared me to death.)

my friends, who did not know what had hapened, screamed and ran. a few seconds later (it seemed like years), they realized i wasn't there and went back. My friends found me and helped me out of the grave. You would not believe how horified and disgusted i felt.

Later we went back to my house and "pigged out" on all the candy. Our adventure was somewhat scarry, but I would definitly do it again.

28

Chapter 3

Building Proofreading Skills in Punctuation

Books and other pieces of writing would be difficult, if not impossible, to read if it were not for punctuation. Punctuation marks are similar to traffic signs. They warn the reader when to *slow down* (comma), when to *stop* (period, question mark, or exclamation mark), and when to be on the *lookout for something interesting or dangerous ahead* (quotation marks, underlining, hyphen, apostrophe, colon, semicolon, or parentheses).

The purpose of this chapter is to develop and improve your punctuation skills in proofreading. Working successfully through the following proofreading exercises will help you improve your punctuation skills.

PRETEST: Proofread the following sentences for end punctuation marks (**period, question mark, and exclamation mark**). Using the proofreading symbols (see page 5), add the appropriate punctuation mark to each sentence.

Sample:
Where is the beautiful vase that Aunt Martha gave me?

1. Sing the song with me so that we can practice for the performance.
2. When did the robin build that nest in the oak tree?
3. That sunset is incredibly exquisite and inspiring! or .
4. Tell Karina to call her house and speak to her mom.
5. Why have you been talking on the phone for two hours?
6. Seventh graders are such an awesome group of young people! or .
7. Did you really enjoy your trip to Oregon?
8. Sit down and begin taking notes on Chapter 14.
9. Wow! What an exciting football game! or .
10. This lunch is one of the best we have had this year. or !

29

Building Proofreading Skills in Punctuation
Period, Question Mark, and Comma

ACTIVITY: Proofread the following exercises for errors in punctuation (**period, question mark, and comma**). Using the proofreading symbols (see page 5), add the correct punctuation.

Rule 1: Use a comma after the salutation of a friendly letter and after the closing of any letter (Dear Mary Lou,).

Rule 2: Use a comma to separate items in dates and addresses (May 3, 1996).

Rule 3: Appositives and appositive phrases are usually set off by commas (Harriett, my best friend,).

Rule 4: An abbreviation is followed by a period (Aug.).

Rule 5: Use a comma to separate city and state (Bangor, Maine).

Samples:

John F. Kennedy   Dr. A. Phillip Jones   Feb. 15, 1983

1. Cofer Bros. Lumber Co. is hiring workers until Sept. 1 for their lumber yard.
2. The private plane was landing at Charlie B. Thomas Airfield during the storm.
3. The minivan was traveling at only 55 mph on the Douglas R. McDonald Freeway.
4. My son Richard was born on Sept. 25, 1987 in Oklahoma City, Oklahoma.
5. Our family visited Springfield, Illinois where President Lincoln practiced law.
6. Did you receive your B.A. degree from Northwestern University?
7.

July 10, 1997

Dear Martha,

We are pleased to invite you to Alicia's birthday party on Friday, July 21, at 3 P.M. at Joe's Pizza Parlor on Memorial Drive.

Sincerely,

Building Proofreading Skills in Punctuation
Comma

ACTIVITY: Proofread the following sentences for errors in comma usage. Using the correct proofreading symbol (see page 5), add commas where necessary.

Rule 1: Use commas to separate words in a series (eggs, milk, and cheese).

Rule 2: Use a comma before *and, but, or, nor, for,* and *yet* when they join independent clauses. (Jim really likes golf, but he doesn't like tennis.)

Rule 3: Parenthetical expressions are set off by commas. (**To be honest,** I thought the book was well written.)

Rule 4: Use commas to set off introductory phrases and clauses. (**Since we have had no rain,** we have watered our lawn every day.)

Rule 5: Use a comma to set off words used in direct address. (**Mr. Johnson,** come to the office immediately.)

Sample:
These bats balls and gloves need to go into the duffel bag.

1. The new girl on the block liked sailing but she did not like biking.
2. Maurice sang danced and played the harmonica for the talent show.
3. Our team if you can believe it won the championship last year.
4. During the Civil War life was very chaotic near the battlefields.
5. Tell me Louise if you can work for me on Thursday evening.
6. Frederick my oldest brother is a leader and motivational speaker.
7. Dad have you heard of this alternative group?
8. When did Francesca my cousin have the time to write a book?
9. Before drawing her brother cleaned his messy room.
10. When she fell down the shaggy dog licked her face.
11. I saw the movie *The Diary of Anne Frank* but I liked the book better.
12. The countries of Italy Mexico France and Russia belong to the United Nations.
13. Our visitor Akiko has returned to her native country Japan.
14. Her birthday June 23 1985 is the same as mine.

Building Proofreading Skills in Punctuation
Comma

ACTIVITY: Using all of the previously stated comma rules, proofread the following sentences for errors. Use the correct proofreading symbols (see page 5) to add commas where they are necessary and to delete commas where they are not necessary. Some sentences may not require any punctuation changes.

Sample:
Elizabeth Taylor was one of the most important movie stars in the 1960s, and now she is a very successful businesswoman in the perfume industry.

1. The famous designer Nell Bennett, will speak today at Macy's at 3:00 P.M.
2. Since I have not completed my research paper on time Mrs. Slaton has given me three days to finish it.
3. If you will help me bake you may have some cookies.
4. You may work on the computer for an hour or you may work on the GeoSafari®.
5. Yes Allen the play *Evita* is one written by Andrew Lloyd Webber.
6. Of course Lori Sandra would be happy to go with you to Sears.
7. Walker's favorite sports are canoeing basketball hiking and swimming.
8. Call me Leland if you can assist at the concession stand.
9. Gustav have you heard of the author Carl Sandburg?
10. We were thirsty and we were hungry.
11. We came to the office early worked hard and left late on Tuesday of last week.
12. In addition your participation in class discussions is a part of your grade.
13. By the way have you ordered your cap and gown for graduation?
14. Please bring to class the following materials: pencil paper ruler colored pencil protractor and your math book.
15. Before Mantoya started running he looked rather pale and tired.
16. If it rains this afternoon we will go to the movies instead.

32

Building Proofreading Skills in Punctuation
Hyphen and Apostrophe

ACTIVITY: Proofread the following sentences for the correct use of the **hyphen** and **apostrophe.** Using the correct proofreading symbols (see page 5), punctuate the following sentences. If no punctuation is required, write **none** in the left margin.

Rule 1: Use a hyphen to divide a word at the end of a line. (The school's air conditioner stopped on the hottest day of the year.)

Rule 2: Use a hyphen with compound numbers from twenty-one to ninety-nine and with fractions used as adjectives (a two-thirds majority of the vote).

Rule 3: To form the possessive case of a singular noun, add an apostrophe and an s (the dog's bone).

Rule 4: To form the possessive case of a plural noun ending in s, add an apostrophe and an s (the students's reports). (There are some exceptions to this rule which you will not need to know for this exercise.)

Rule 5: Use an apostrophe to show where letters have been omitted in a contraction. (We'll sing several campfire songs.)

Sample:
Did you find the doctors bag in his car?

1. When did the Millers dog run away from home?
2. Isnt that Andrews black cat that I saw in the street?
3. Bobs new car was traveling at seventy-five miles per hour.
4. Many animals homes are destroyed when rain forests are cut down.
5. My mother-in-law lives in the South American country of Bolivia.
6. Its too soon for the childrens toys to be broken.
7. The woodworking book has a beautiful design on its cover.
8. Marianne paid ninety-nine cents for a one-half pound bag of peanuts.
9. I wonder whether or not the young driver of that red Corvette is going to precede us or follow us to the cemetery.
10. Naturally the four-cylinder car engine was much faster than the two-cylinder one.
11. The current president and vice president won reelection by a three-fourths majority.

BONUS:
Write five sentences with mistakes using hyphens and apostrophes. Then give your paper to a classmate to proofread.

33

Building Proofreading Skills in Punctuation
Semicolon and Colon

ACTIVITY: Proofread the following sentences for the correct usage of the **semicolon** and **colon.** Use the proofreading symbols (see page 5) to add semicolons and hyphens where necessary.

Rule 1: Use a semicolon between independent clauses in a sentence if they are not joined by *and, but, nor, for,* or *yet.*

Rule 2: Use a semicolon between independent clauses joined by such words as *for example, besides, nevertheless, therefore, however,* and *instead.*

Rule 3: A semicolon (rather than a comma) may be needed to separate the independent clauses of a compound sentence if commas appear within the clauses.

Rule 4: Use a colon before a list of items, especially after expressions such as *the following* or *as follows.*

Rule 5: Use a colon between the hour and minute when writing the time.

Rule 6: Use a colon after the salutation of a business letter.

Sample:
The garage, living room, kitchen, and dining room are on the first floor the bedrooms and bathrooms are on the second floor.

1. On our first trip to Disneyworld, we wanted to see Epcot Center my little sister wanted to stay in the Magic Kingdom.
2. Our favorite sights and rides at Disneyworld included the following the Teacups, Magic Mountain, and the Disney Parade.
3. Our family enjoyed many different foods while we visited the Magic Kingdom Mexican, Polynesian, and French.
4. My friends enjoy playing many different games however, we play some games over and over checkers, chess, and video games.
5. I have many favorite songs one of my favorite songs is from the movie *Waiting to Exhale.*
6. We arrived at the party exactly at 8:30 P.M. and left at 11:25 P.M.
7. She disliked so many of her chores cleaning up her room, washing the dishes, emptying the trash, and taking care of her cat.
8. Dear Mrs. Caldwell   Dear Sir   Gentlemen
9. Jay raised horses, cows, and rabbits he really enjoyed caring for the horses.
10. I have never forgotten my grandfather's advice My son, once you tell one lie, you often have to tell more lies to cover up the first one.

©1999 by Incentive Publications, Inc.
Nashville, TN.

Building Proofreading Skills in Punctuation
Quotation Marks and Underlining

ACTIVITY: Proofread the following sentences for the correct usage of **quotation marks** and **underlining (or italics)**. Using the correct proofreading symbols (see page 5), add quotation marks and underlining where necessary.

Rule 1: Use underlining (or *italics*) for titles of books, periodicals, works of art, plays, films, ships, and the like.

Rule 2: Use quotation marks to enclose a direct quotation (a person's exact words).

Rule 3: A direct quotation is set off from the rest of the sentence by commas or by a question mark or exclamation point.

Rule 4: A period or a comma following a quotation should be placed *inside* the closing quotation marks. A period is only used if the quotation comes at the end of the sentence that includes it.

Rule 5: A question mark or an exclamation point should be placed *inside* the closing quotation marks if the quotation is a question or an exclamation. Otherwise, it should be placed *outside* the closing quotation marks.

Rule 6: Use quotation marks to enclose titles of short works (poems, short stories, songs, television programs, and articles).

Sample:
Marcia replied, I couldn't read the book, The Friendship, because my dog ate it.

1. Did you see that beautiful hot air balloon? called Francis.
2. Jurassic Park by Michael Crichton is one of my favorite books.
3. My mother said angrily, Get your hair cut today or suffer the consequences!
4. Have you read Call of the Wild by Jack London, Pierre asked, the story of a dog and a boy?
5. All of my friends really enjoyed the article Denzel Washington, The Movie Star, in the recent issue of Ebony.
6. Blaine, Tiffany, and Matt all exclaimed, Planet Hollywood is so awesome!
7. Zachary told us in confidence that he was afraid of ghost stories.
8. Robert Frost's poem Stopping By the Woods on a Snowy Evening is one of my favorites.
9. Yes, Ms. McCoy, I did cheat on my math test that we took last week on Chapter 11, said Juanita.
10. Six Flags over Texas, said Barbara, has many exciting rides and attractions.
11. On our trip to Paris, we visited the Louvre where we saw the Mona Lisa; the most exciting part of our trip was when we returned on the Queen Elizabeth II.

Building Proofreading Skills in Punctuation
Cumulative Review
Spelling, Capitalization, and Punctuation

ACTIVITY: Proofread the following letter for errors in **spelling, capi... ...nctuation.** Use the proofreading symbols (see page 5) to co... ...capitalization errors and to add or delete punctuation wher... ...e sentences may not require any corrections.

Answers may vary

2917 Bristol Way N.E.
Atlanta, Georgia 30309
September 12, 1996

Mrs. Lawanda Greene, President
Acme Publishing Company
448 Larchment Boulevard
Baton Rouge, Lousana 70805

Dear Mrs. Greene:

We will be delighted to welcome your neice Marlene as one of our writers when she moves to Atlanta, as you outlined in your recent letter. Marlene's background in creative writing sounds extremly encouraging for our new series of books entitled Mysteries of the World. When you said, Marlene was one of the most dynamic writers in her class of seventy-five students, I was most impressed. We all feel fortunate to have Marlene join our team of writers.

To speed the process of employment records for our Human Resources department, please ask Marlene to complete the following application, state and federal forms, insurance forms, and documentation forms. could you ask her to also bring her social security card so that we will be able to make a copy of it?

Our entire staff at Bristol Publishing looks forward to greeting Marlene.

Sincerly,

Constance Bristol, President

CB/tm

Building Proofreading Skills in Punctuation
Cumulative Review
Spelling, Capitalization, and Punctuation

ACTIVITY: Proofread the following report, "The Universe" by Conrad Li... spelling, capitalization, and punctuation. Use the p... ...ols (see page 5) to correct all errors.

Answers may vary

The Universe
by Conrad Lisco

have you ever wondered what is out in the universe, there are things out there that we have never seen, things that are just waiting to be discovered, there may be new plants, stars, moons, or even more galaxis.

before technology was improved, people thought the stars were just shining objects in the sky, the ancient roman and greek civilizations made up wonderful myths about gods and goddesses, they were supposedly responsible for creating the universe, and the varous constellations were named after them as were the planets, galileo was able to develop a quite simple telscope by first making a "spyglass" similar to the ones that were around in 1608, in 1610, galileo was able to see the plant jupiter and some of its moons, even with his telscope, the stars and most planets were quite out of reach, at that time, the peple of the seventeenth century thought that galileo's telscope was a great invention.

much later, scientists invented new ways to discover the stars, philosophers developed theories and many new ideas arose, still people could not totally understand the universe, the moon and other planets were now coming closer into view.

since the launching of sputnik (means "traveling companion" in russian) in 1957, many changes have taken place, now we have great machines and people who can acomplish grat feats in science, there are space shuttles like the challenger, satelites such as voyager and the space station Mir (means "peace" in russian), today we can say that we have gotten a closer look at the universe than ever before.

In conclusion, over the years people have struggled to unlock the mysteries of the universe, still today, we strive for the stars and dream of space travel to the planets in our solar system and others.

Building Proofreading Skills in Punctuation
Cumulative Review
Spelling, Capitalization, and Punctuation

ACTIVITY: Proofread the following poem, "A Poison Tree" by William Blake. Using the proofreading symbols (see page 5), correct all errors in **spelling, capitalization, and punctuation.**

A Poison Tree
by William Blake

I was angry with my friend:
I told my wrath, my wrath did end.
I was angry with my foe:
I told it not, my wrath did grow.

And I watered it in fears,
night and morning with my tears;
And I sunned it with smiles,
And with soft deceitful wiles.

And it grew both day and niht,
Till it bore an Apple bright.
And my foe beheld it shine,
And he knew that it was mine.

and into my garden stole
When the night had veiled the pole;*
In the Morning glad I see
My foe outstretced beneath the tree.

*pole: sky

Building Proofreading Skills in Punctuation
Cumulative Review
Punctuation and Capitalization

ACTIVITY: Proofread the following school announcement for errors in punctuation and capitalization. Use the proofreading symbols (see page 5) to correct the mistakes. Copy the corrected announcement on a separate piece of paper.

INTERNATIONAL CELEBRATION

Parents and friends of briarcliff middle school, we cordially invite you to celebrate our Third Annual International Dinner on march 15,1997. This celebration of our Cultural Diversity involves an entire week to honor our heritage from many lands, many backgrounds, and many languages.

Last year when the PTA led us in a festival of redecoration, we hung flags and banners from twenty-one different countries. many classes decorated flags to honor countries they had studied. Families also sponsored or purchased flags to honor their homelands, and their new school. In almost every class, students learned interesting facts about each country, and studied the language of a particular country.

For this years week long celebration we invite parents and friends to participate in one of the following ways: teach a craft, cook a special dish, share or teach a dance, or speak to individual classes about your homeland. If you are interested in helping, please contact Marilyn Van derber at (440) 741-1234 after 7:00 P.M.

Join us for our Third Annual International Dinner on March 15, 1997 at 6:00 P.M. in the Briarcliff Middle School Cafeteria. Families should bring dishes from their homelands. The pta will provide the soft drinks and paper products. Our keynote speaker will be the well-known storyteller Carmen Fiedlo. For reservations, please call Dr. Theodore Washburn at (440) 741-7890 before March 10, 1997.

SPECIAL NOTE: There are about 35 corrections needed in the above announcement. Did you find all of the errors? If not, reread the announcement to see if you can find the errors you missed.

Building Proofreading Skills in Language Usage
Parts of Speech

ACTIVITY: Proofread the following list of **adjectives, nouns, verbs, adverbs, prepositions, conjunctions, and interjections.** Each item below gives four possible choices for the part of speech listed. Choose the word that is an example of the **part of speech** listed in the first column. Circle the letter of the correct answer.

Sample:

adjective	(a.) softest	b. tightly	c. quickly	d. against
1. adverb	a. haunted	b. catching	c. ouch	(d.) slightly
2. preposition	a. what	b. quietly	(c.) between	d. approach
3. conjunction	(a.) but	b. goodness	c. below	d. are
4. interjection	a. drove	b. noisily	(c.) oops	d. uncertain
5. verb	a. growth	b. tulip	c. she	(d.) wishing
6. adjective	a. reach	(b.) vacant	c. quarrel	d. girl
7. adverb	(a.) clearly	b. clear	c. nor	d. without
8. conjunction	a. any	b. several	c. would	(d.) and
9. preposition	a. round	(b.) around	c. distant	d. running
10. pronoun	a. wish	b. Rocky	(c.) him	d. wishing
11. noun	(a.) swimsuit	b. swam	c. splashed	d. soapy
12. adjective	a. bought	b. belong	c. bother	(d.) beautiful
13. pronoun	a. there	(b.) their	c. three	d. thus
14. preposition	(a.) aboard	b. board	c. bored	d. abound
15. verb	a. slippery	b. studious	(c.) prepared	d. conductor
16. adjective	a. over	b. from	(c.) several	d. cartoon
17. interjection	a. wonder	b. greatly	c. visited	(d.) goodness

Building Proofreading Skills in Language Usage
Troublesome Verbs (sit and set; rise and raise; lie and lay)

ACTIVITY: Carefully proofread the following sentences for errors in using the six **troublesome verbs (sit and set; rise and raise; lie and lay).** Decide if the italicized verb has been used correctly in the sentence. If it has not, use the proofreading symbols (see page 5) to correct the verb.

Rule 1: Use a form of **sit (sit, sat, sitting)** when you mean "to rest in a sitting position." (*She sat patiently waiting for the Olympic runners.*) Use a form of **set (set, sets, setting)** when you mean "to put or place" something. (*Kennedy set the dinner table for four special guests.*)

Rule 2: Use a form of **rise (rise, rose, risen)** when you mean "to ascend, to swell up, and to rise in value or force." (*We waited for the dough to rise.*) Use a form of **raise (raise, raised, raised)** when you mean "to lift up, to cause it to go up, or to increase in amount." (*Stanley raised the flag.*)

Rule 3: Use a form of **lie (lie, lay, lain, lying)** when you mean "to rest or recline." (*Susanna has been lying on the chaise lounge all afternoon.*) Use a form of **lay (lay, laid, laying)** when you mean "to put or place" something. (*Josephine has been laying bathroom tiles in a unique pattern.*)

Sample:
By early morning Nikki had rose *(risen)* high in his hot air balloon.

1. You may borrow my thesaurus, which is *laying (lying)* on the floor next to the sofa.
2. Mother asked Sandra to *sit (set)* the table before the guests arrived.
3. Because Tommy has been sick, he must *lay (lie)* down and rest for one hour.
4. She thought that she had *lain (laid)* the briefcase on the front seat of her car.
5. After we had been *setting (sitting)* there for almost an hour, we learned the bus had left us.
6. Scarlet carefully *lay (laid)* out the gown that she was wearing to the dance.
7. After a delicious dinner, we *set (sat)* down to play a trivia game.
8. The distinguished speaker slowly *raised (rose)* to the podium.
9. Fabio was *lying (laying)* the tiles in the new bathroom.
10. When I walked past the office, Tommy was *setting (sitting)* in the chair next to the principal.
11. (no item)
12. Many of my classmates have *lain (lain)* awake at night after reading one of Poe's stories.

Building Proofreading Skills in Language Usage
Subject-Verb Agreement

ACTIVITY: Proofread the following sentences for errors in **subject-verb agreement.** Use the proofreading symbols (see page 5) to correct the verb in each sentence.

Rule: The subject and verb of a sentence must agree in number. A singular subject requires a singular verb, and a plural subject requires a plural verb.
Singular: *The state bird of Georgia is the Brown Thrasher.*
Plural: *The candidates have all qualified for the upcoming election.*

Sample:
The hamster were *(was)* in his cage all night long.

1. Marvin and Lillian visits *(visit)* New York every spring.
2. Peoria, Illinois are *(is)* a wonderful, quiet place to raise a family.
3. The majority of the Russian voters is *(are)* voting in the presidential election today.
4. The dark-haired girl were *(was)* chosen for the Miss America contest in her local pageant.
5. The cherry tomatoes in my dad's garden grow *(grows)* rapidly.
6. My new black cocker spaniel run *(runs)* away every time I call him.
7. The palm trees on the Caribbean island sway *(sways)* in the wind all day long.
8. The experienced pitcher throw *(throws)* the ball in a variety of ways.
9. The beautifully colored macaw have *(has)* an extremely powerful beak.
10. The assistant principal of our school award *(awards)* certificates for attendance.
11. The Aztecs was *(were)* conquered by the Spanish after much bloodshed.
12. She lie *(lies)* on the dirty floor of the newly renovated basement.
13. The candidate shake *(shakes)* hands with as many voters as she can.

BONUS:
Write a passage in which some subjects and verbs do not agree; then, give it to a classmate to proofread.

Building Proofreading Skills in Language Usage
Sentence Fragments

ACTIVITY: Proofread the following for **sentence fragments.** (Remember that fragments are pieces of sentences punctuated as if they were complete sentences.) Circle S if the group of words is a complete sentence, and circle F if the group of words is a fragment. Then, rewrite the fragments to make a complete sentence.

Sample:
   S ⓕ   Wimbledon, one of the most important tennis tournaments.

1. ⓢ F   Ms. Moody told her class to divide up into small groups.
2. S ⓕ   Coretta Scott King, the widow of Dr. Martin Luther King.
3. ⓢ F   While Terry was on vacation, his car caused him a lot of trouble.
4. S ⓕ   As I was slowly driving home from the movies.
5. S ⓕ   Having been given the signal to start the games.
6. ⓢ F   His older sisters always treated him so cruelly.
7. S ⓕ   Waiting patiently at the dentist office for several hours.
8. ⓢ F   I simply do not understand why he does not go to the doctor.
9. S ⓕ   When we moved last summer to San Diego.
10. ⓢ F   Please open your books to page 115.
11. ⓢ F   At the bottom of page 115, you will notice two exercises.
12. S ⓕ   Who always complain about the cafeteria meals.
13. S ⓕ   Offering additional classes in Spanish for all seventh-graders.
14. ⓢ F   Learning to operate a computer is quite an accomplishment.
15. ⓢ F   Josh considered running for seventh-grade president.

BONUS:
Write a paragraph containing several sentence fragments. Give it to a classmate to proof-read and correct.

Building Proofreading Skills in Language Usage
Pronoun-Antecedent Agreement

ACTIVITY: Every pronoun refers to another word, which is called its **antecedent.** Whenever you use a pronoun, make sure that it agrees with its antecedent in number and gender.
Proofread the following sentences for errors in **pronoun–antecedent agreement.** Use the proofreading symbols (see page 5) for omitting and inserting a word to correct the sentences. Some sentences may not need any corrections.

Sample:
   Everyone in Mrs. Slaton's class gave their [his or her] report on space exploration.

1. No one on the committee gave their [his or her] approval on the upcoming issue.
2. Each of the newspapers has had the governor's picture on its front page.
3. Several others, including Ben, volunteered to present his [theirs] first.
4. The science book had Bryan's name written inside their [its] cover.
5. Neither the father nor the son had remembered to bring its [his] tool kit.
6. Nobody in the fifth period class would admit to their [his or her] low test score.
7. In most cases, a cat or a dog that becomes lost in the deep woods can easily take care of themselves [itself].
8. Nadia and Keshia wore her [their] cheerleader uniforms to the practice today.
9. A few of my neighbors have installed watering systems in their yards.
10. One of my goofy relatives always wears their [his or her] tennis shoes without strings.

Building Proofreading Skills in Language Usage
Run-On Sentences

ACTIVITY: Run-on sentences are two or more sentences that "run together" without a period separating them. Remember, run-on sentences sometimes have commas separating them.
Proofread the following passage for run-on sentences. Use the proofreading symbols (see page 5) to correct the run-ons. Remember to start each new sentence with a capital letter and to end each with the proper punctuation mark.

Sample: There are five themes of geography one of the themes is *location.*

Location refers to the position of people and places on the earth's surface the exact position or absolute location of something on the earth's surface can be identified by using lines of longitude and latitude. Relative location is the relationship of one place to other places people think about such relationships when they decide where to live, where to work, or where to build a school.

Another geographic theme is *place* three fundamental characteristics give identity to a place and distinguish it from other places: physical characteristics, human characteristics, and image. Physical characteristics include landforms, bodies of water, climate, soils, natural vegetation, and animal life. Human characteristics, however, include buildings, farms, and other human environments that people create.

Human-environment interaction is another geographic theme different people use the natural environment in different ways people often modify the natural environment to meet their needs when humans interact with the natural environment, consequences always exist some are intended others are not.

Relationships between people in different places constitute the fourth geographic theme, *movement*—the movement of people, goods, and ideas people travel from one place to another often people in one place have goods that people in another place want. The people in these two places are potential trading partners.

A *region,* the fifth and final geographic theme, is an area that has some unifying characteristics they are convenient and manageable for organizing our knowledge of the world there are many ways to define a region, depending on the issues or problems being considered. The criteria used to define regions can be physical, human, or both.

Building Proofreading Skills in Language Usage
Dangling and Misplaced Modifiers

ACTIVITY: A **dangling** or **misplaced modifier** changes the meaning of a sentence or makes it unclear or nonsensical because the modifying phrase is in the wrong place.
Proofread the following sentences to find the **dangling** or **misplaced modifiers.** First, underline the dangling or misplaced modifiers. Then, using proofreading circles, arrows, and transpose symbols (see page 5) show where the phrase belongs. You may need to add or change some words and to correct capitalization and punctuation, as well.

Answers may vary

Sample: At the age of six Foluke's mom took him to the zoo. (tr)

1. Pacing the floor angrily my cellular phone was ringing while I was. (tr)
2. Many people often avoid walking under ladders who are superstitious. (tr)
3. I saw Dontavius Lott run fifty yards for a touchdown while eating a hot dog and drinking a coke. (tr)
4. Isaac thought about his problems riding a bicycle and singing a song. (tr)
5. Staying at the beach house all summer, while I was the sun-block supply was depleted. (tr)
6. After I walked walking up the hill, the bucket had to be lowered into the well.
7. Father baked a two-layer cake for the birthday party that was dripping strawberry frosting. (tr)
8. The audience gave a standing ovation when Deontae finished his piano performance in the balcony. (tr)
9. The acorns were crushed by the tractor lying on the ground. (tr)
10. The typist finished her work and began to drive home then drove at her desk. (tr)
11. Swimming perfectly, who swam a gold medal was won by Amy at the Summer Olympics in Atlanta. (tr)

BONUS:
Write several sentences in which the word order sounds wrong or makes the meaning unclear. First, proofread the sentences yourself to be sure that each can be corrected. Then, give the uncorrected sentences to a classmate to proofread.

Panel 47

47

Building Proofreading Skills in Language Usage
Comparitive Forms of Adjectives and Adverbs

ACTIVITY: Proofread the following sentences for errors in the comparitive forms of adjectives and adverbs. Use the proofreading symbols (see page 5) to rewrite the adjective or adverb, using the correct degree of comparison.

> **Rule 1:** When you are comparing two things (*comparative degree*), add the suffix *-er* to most one-syllable modifiers (*stronger*). If the modifier has two or more syllables, then use the word *more* or *less* (*more clever, less likely*).
>
> **Rule 2:** When you are comparing three or more things (*superlative degree*), add the suffix *-est* to most one-syllable modifiers (*warmest*). If the modifier has two or more syllables, then use the word *most* or *least* (*most dependable, least reliable*).

Sample:
That was the greatest movie I have ever seen.

1. The magician had to perform the most difficult magic tricks of all the performers.
2. The magician's assistant, Maria, was the most beautiful of all the performers in the show.
3. The second act of the show was the least exciting of all the performances.
4. Children seemed to enjoy the performance of the bears best of all.
5. Special effects were used more effectively than they were previously.
6. Lynn completed her science project earlier than anyone else in her class.
7. For the Invent America Contest, Tom created the most fascinating creations.
8. This math problem was the most difficult of all the problems we've had this year.
9. The lion is considered to be one of the fiercest animals in the grassland of Kenya.
10. She worked harder than the other mechanic at the automotive center.

Panel 48

48

Building Proofreading Skills in Language Usage
Double Negatives

ACTIVITY: Words such as *no, not, none, never, no one, nothing, scarcely,* and ____ called negatives. (Many negatives begin with the letter n.) Negative ____ andard English require only one negative word. Use of more tha ____ ord is called a double negative. (*We do not have no ho ____ w.*) Always avoid the use of double negatives.

Using the proofreading symbol for deleting (see ____ ge 5), first delete the double negative. Then rewrite each sentence correctly on the line provided.

Sample:
Too much homework doesn't scarcely leave time to watch television.
Too much homework doesn't leave time to watch television.

1. Rosie said, "I don't want no one on my show with a bad attitude."
   Rosie said, "I don't want anyone on my show with a bad attitude."
2. Your answer to the math problem doesn't make no sense to me.
   Your answer to the math problem doesn't make sense to me.
3. I don't know nothing about our state's history or its government.
   I don't know anything about our state's history or its government.
4. George hasn't never been to the Black Hills of South Dakota.
   George hasn't been to the Black Hills of South Dakota.
5. The candidate told the reporters that she would not have no comment.
   The candidate told the reporters that she would not have any comment.
6. Johnny's mother could not hardly believe she had won the state lottery.
   Johnny's mother could not believe she had won the state lottery.
7. Don't never use "none" and "nothing" in the same sentence.
   Don't use "none" and "nothing" in the same sentence.
8. I didn't receive no notice about my failing grade in English.
   I didn't receive notice about my failing grade in English.

BONUS:
Write several sentences using double negatives. Then, exchange your paper with a classmate to proofread.

Panel 49

49

Building Proofreading Skills in Language Usage
Cumulative Review
Spelling, Capitalization, Punctuation, and Language Usage

ACTIVITY: Correct the errors in spelling, capitalization, punctua ____ agreement, sentence fragments, run-on sentences, dangli ____ modifiers, and double negatives from Isabelle McCoy's tru ____ ay of the Bubbles." Use the proofreading symbols (see page 5) to m ____ er corrections.

The Day of the Bubbles

When my brother Edward was a young boy, only about four, he followed my Mom around as she did her work. We lived in a two-story house with a full basement. In the basement was the washing machine and a large play area. My brother would play while my mom worked with his train and other toys.

One day while she was doing the laundry and working on supper upstairs, my brother obviously became bored and wanted to try something new. He got the box of detergeant and was going to use it for who knows what. It spilled and there was detergeant all over the floor. Seeing the mess and not wanting to get into trouble, my brother naturally did what any four-year old would do. He tried to cover it up, but it was a large spill. He looked for the broom, but it was not in sight. What he did see was the hose that my mom used to scrub the floor of the basement. Now my brother had watched my mom do this many times. So he decided he wanted to wash the floor. He got the hose and turned on the water. Unfortunately, he turned on the water full blast and there right before his eyes, a mound of soap bubbles began to form. Wow, he said. This is great—bubbles, just like in the bathtub, but no bath.

Panel 50

50

The Day of the Bubbles, continued

He of course promptly forgot that he was trying not to get in trouble for spilling the detergeant. Edward began to slip and slide through the bubbles. His squeals of delight carried upstairs to the kitchen. Mom went to the head of the stairs and called to my brother, "What are you doing?"

His reply was just what you or I would say if we were caught doing something wrong.

He said, "I'm not doing anything, Mommy."

My mother, being the intelligent person that she is, didn't believe him for an instant. She proceeded to investigate. Reaching the bottom step, giggling and the sound of water running she heard. As mom turned the corner, she was just in time to see my brother standing amid a large mound of bubbles. Needless to say my mom was not too happy. Her roast was cooking and my dad would be home soon. She did not have any time to deal with this mess.

Mother said, "Edward come here!"

Like an "ideal" four-year-old child, caught being bad, he replied, "No!"

My mom was very angry. And took a step toward my brother. She didn't realize that the floor would be so slippery and her feet went out from under her. Mom slides across the floor, feet first. Edward thought she was joining in on the fun, and he slides the other way. After trying to catch him several times, mom stopped and sat on the floor. My brother made another slide through the bubbles and landed in her lap. By this time my mother's anger had turned to laughter.

©1999 by Incentive Publications, Inc.
Nashville, TN.

Proofreading for Clarity, Transition, and Order

By now you have learned to proofread for a variety of errors: spelling, capitalization, punctuation, parts of speech, subject-verb agreement, sentence fragments, run-on sentences, dangling and misplaced modifiers, comparison of adjectives and adverbs, pronoun-antecedent agreement, and double negatives. The lessons in this chapter involve more ~~~~ on paragraphing, word order, transitions, sentence variety, wordiness, ~~~~ ~~~~ sentences. Each activity will give you practice in all areas of ~~~~ helping you write any assignment more successfully.

Answers may vary

ACTIVITY: Review of proofreading marks. In the space next to each proofreading mark, write what the mark means. Then, on the second line, give an example of how the symbol is used.

Sample:

b̲ _Capitalize a lowercase letter_
Example: _be on time for cheerleading practice._

⌃ 1. _Add a comma._
Example: _While I was waiting for the bus, I saw an accident._

⌒ 2. _Close up space._
Example: _Some one will assist you with your selections_

⊘ 3. _Use a lower-case letter_
Example: _My Brother Bob graduated with honors._

⊙ 4. _Add a period._
Example: _Please ask Dr Harrison for a hall pass._

∼ 5. _Change the order of letters or words._
Example: _In the rush of leaving, forgot he his keys._

Proofreading for Clarity, Transition, and Order
Review of Proofreading Marks. Continued

Answers may vary

¶ 6. _Begin a new paragraph._
Example: _¶ Mr. Williams read the school rules._

∨⌃ 7. _Add or insert a missing word, letter, or punctuation mark._
Example: _Susie read her short story to the class._

:| 8. _Add a colon._
Example: _The business letter read| Dear Mr. Walker:|_

tr 9. _Move the circled words to the place marked by the arrow._
Example: _The boys threw, for cows hay over the fence tr_

℮ 10. _Delete a word, letter, or punctuation mark._
Example: _Jamie gave too to many reasons for not coming._

11. _Add a space._
Example: _The oldman rocked on his porch all day._

∨"∨ 12. _Insert quotation marks._
Example: _Elaine quickly said, Stay out of that cookie jar!_

sp 13. _Spell out_
Example: _The clerk mistakenly cut 20 twenty inches too much._

stet 14. _Let marked text stay as written._
Example: _My mother was extremely disgusted with him. stet_

✓ 15. _Add an apostrophe._
Example: _Thomas showed me his brother's new computer_

Proofreading for Clarity, Transition, and Order
Sentence Order

Answers may vary

ACTIVITY: When we write, it is important to make sure that our ideas are written ~~~~ sible order. In the following paragraphs, the sentences are out of ~~~~ ~~~~ rder of the sentences by writing the number *1* at the beginning ~~~~ the first sentence, the number *2* at the beginning of the ~~~~ and so on. In case you change your mind, use a pencil so that ~~~~ ~~~~ when you have finished, read the sentences aloud in the order in whi~~~~ ~~~~ renumbered them. Finally, write the three paragraphs on a clean sheet of ~~~~ per.

Remember: A paragraph should begin with a topic sentence that tells the general idea of the paragraph.

1. ② The Egyptians had stools, chairs, chests, tables, and beds, examples of which can be seen in museums today. ⑥ They also painted scenes of everyday life on the walls of the tombs. Many centuries later, when the sealed tombs were opened, examples of both the real furniture and the furniture painted on the walls ③ were found. The origin of furniture as we know it goes back to ancient Egypt. They put such everyday objects in their tombs. Some of these were indoor scenes that showed an abundance of furniture.

2. In fact, these contests were often the main events at country fairs. ② We all know the story of Robin Hood and his band of merry archers who roamed Sherwood Forest. ① The sport of archery has long been associated with tales of romance and valor. ③ We know, too, of William Tell, whose skill with a bow saved his life. ④ Many a tale set in early England tells of picturesque and colorful archery contests.

3. About sixty years later, a railroad connected the two cities, and, by the twentieth century, fast planes and automobiles had been developed. By 1775, horse-drawn coaches had lessened the time to two days. In less than three hundred years, the ever-increasing speed of travel has completely changed our ideas of distance. In 1675, the normal way to travel from New York City to Philadelphia was on foot, and the trip took three to five days. ⑤ Now we can cover the distance in a few minutes by jet.

Proofreading for Clarity, Transition, and Order
Sentence Order. Continued

4. ⑥ Today, over twenty-two billion tin cans are used to store packed food. ⑤ As long ago as 55 B.C., the early Romans coated copper vessels with tin to make them suitable as food containers. ② A tin can, first of all, has very little tin in it. ① Everyone uses tin cans, but few people know much about them. ④ Coating a metal with tin is a process that has been known a long time. ③ The can is made of tin plate that is over 98% steel with only a coating of tin.

5. ① There are three important actions that students can take to save energy. ⑥ For example, I noticed a newspaper article last week about opening a bus lane on Decatur Street. Last evening at home, I counted five lights that were left on needlessly. ⑤ We should support this idea in our letters. At home, we can turn off lights that are not in use. ② Finally, when we travel to the mall, to the skating rink, or to other places with friends, we should use public transportation, such as buses, subways, and trains. At school, we can write letters to public officials, reminding them of how important it is to conserve energy whenever possible. ④ I promptly turned them off.

Proofreading for Clarity, Transition, and Order
55
Word Order within Sentences

ACTIVITY: Writers often change the order of words in sentences to make the meaning clearer. Often they edit to make a sentence flow more effectively. To do this, writers use proofreading symbols such as circles, arrows, transpose marks, and so forth (see page 5).

Proofread the sentences below and correct them by using the appropriate proofreading symbols. You may need to add or delete words.

Sample:

I read about the lost kitten that was found in today's newspaper.

1. Pass me the mashed potatoes and gravy please. (tr)
2. We saw the trapeze artist swinging dangerously through our binoculars. (tr)
3. Coming in for a landing the air traffic controller radioed the plane. (tr)
4. Jogging down the sidewalk my puppy followed me. (tr)
5. My toddler crawled into my lap reading a book. (tr)
6. To read books in the media center is a wonderful place. (tr)
7. The lake the students ate their picnic lunch down by. (tr)
8. My married brother Joseph came for the weekend to see me who lives in Wyoming. (tr)
9. The jacket belongs to my best friend that I have lost.
10. Walking through Central Park the chipmunks chattered at me. (tr)
11. Our family watched the snow pile up in drifts inside our warm home. (tr)
12. Destroyed by the fire the man looked sadly at the charred house. (tr)
13. The messenger gave Mr. Holland two dozen balloons who was dressed as a duck. (tr)
14. We quietly tiptoed over the ice in our heavy boots which had begun to crack. (tr)

BONUS:

Write at least four sentences in which the word order is unclear or sounds incorrect. Proofread them yourself to make sure that the sentences can be rewritten. Then, give the incorrect sentences to a classmate to proofread.

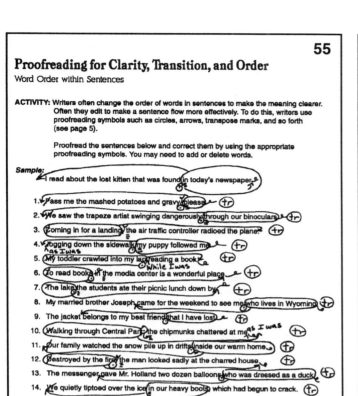

Proofreading for Clarity, Transition, and Order
56
Transition

ACTIVITY: Many writers fail to take the reader smoothly from one idea to the next. This move from one idea to the next is called **transition**. The most common transitional words are: *as, since, because, after, before, next, then, although, therefore, after, and, but, for ,also, so, while,* and *thus.* Proofread the following paragraph, and use the appropriate proofreading symbols (see page 5) to add the appropriate transitional words when necessary. You may combine sentences and add words if needed. Then, on a separate sheet of paper, rewrite the corrected paragraph.

Sample:

Our Persian cat is quite finicky. She eats only albacore tuna.

Our Persian cat is quite finicky; therefore, she eats only albacore tuna.

The beekeeper had a clever way of finding wild bees. He was carrying a small wooden box with a sliding cover. He would go to a meadow. He would find a bee in a flower and capture it in his box. He would pull back the cover and release the bee. He knew that the pollen-laden insect would return to the tree where the wild bees were gathered. He would carefully record the direction of flight. He would move to the other side of the meadow. He would capture another bee. He would release it. He would record the direction in which it flew. He knew that both bees would head home by the most direct route. He knew that the cluster of bees must be found at the point where his imaginary lines crossed. It was easy to capture the swarm in a large net and move it to his own orchard. The beekeeper was simply using mathematics.

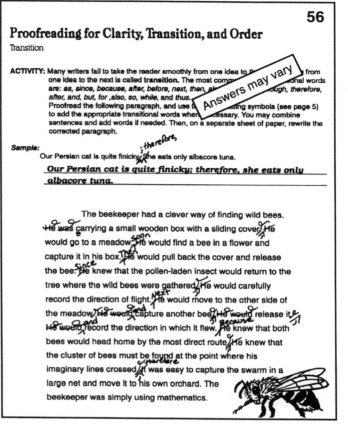

Answers may vary

Proofreading for Clarity, Transition, and Order
57
Sentence Variety

ACTIVITY: When we write, most of us have a problem with stringing together words and ideas into a single sentence. Most good writers will have a variety of sentences—some long and some short. One of the best rules to follow is to *read aloud* what you have written.

In the following exercise, you are the editor. Use the proofreading symbols, edit the passage below to create sentence variety. You will need to add and delete words as well as change punctuation and capitalization. Then, on a separate sheet of paper, rewrite the corrected paragraph.

Sample:

Dr. Harris Bergman spoke to the audience. He spoke with great conviction.

With great conviction, Dr. Harris Bergman spoke to the audience.

Marie and Ellen had colds when they visited their aunt in Hollywood but they remember the stay as a very exciting time, for they took an afternoon bus tour past the big homes of the movie stars they shopped on Hollywood Boulevard they couldn't come home without presents for the family and then Marie went alone to see a live television talk show and Ellen spent a day in bed to shake off her cold but the next day Marie stayed in bed for the same reason and Ellen went to a crowded movie premiere at Grauman's Chinese Theater and on the last day of their visit their aunt took them to Disneyland.

Answers may vary

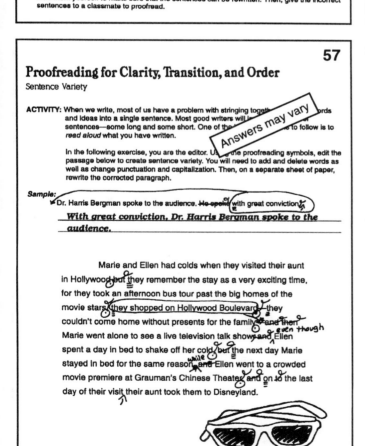

Proofreading for Clarity, Transition, and Order
58
Wordiness

ACTIVITY: Writers often use needless extra words—this is called **wordiness**. As you read, make your writing crisper and, therefore, more interesting by deleting unnecessary words. In the following passage, delete any extra words by using the proper proofreading symbols. You may even want to delete the needless words and replace them with only one word.

Sample:

I like to think of my brother as a genius because he scored an 800 on the math section of the SAT, and he went to Harvard and he scored an 800 on the verbal section.

Not Born a Genius
by Kermit Finch

In order for you to become a genius, you have to work for it because you are not born with a gift that lets you know everything there is to know instantly, however you can be born with a high IQ and still not be a genius. A classic example is Albert Einstein, who could be called a genius, but he had to work at it. If you want to be a genius, you have to set your goal on it.

I read a story about this "brain child" who was writing computer programs when he was only four years old so he must have been talking at three months of age, and I think the title for him is "kid genius." I don't think he was born knowing everything, but he just had a very, very high IQ.

In my opinion, a genius is someone who has very high intellect and a better understanding of the world, but there is no doubt in my mind that a person has to work hard to become a genius. One of the smartest inventors, for instance Benjamin Franklin, performed poorly in school, but he invented many things. It is a fact that very many intelligent people perform very poorly in their academic work.

In summary, there are no guarantees that you will without a doubt become a genius even though you may have a notably extremely high IQ.

Answers may vary

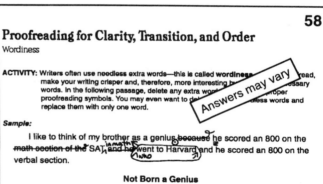

Proofreading for Clarity, Transition, and Order
Combining Sentences

ACTIVITY: Some writers string too many words and ideas together in one sentence ~~Answers may vary~~ writing is composed of a variety of effective sentences—some l~~ong~~ short. Sentences should not just "bump along;" instead, senten~~ces~~ ~~should read~~ smoothly from word to word, phrase to phrase, and idea to id~~ea~~ ~~Effective~~ sentences will make you a more proficient, successful w~~riter~~ Create more effective sentences for the items ~~below~~ by rewriting the sentences according to the directions given for each.

Sample:

During half time, Coach Williams gave the players confidence in themselves. The players were deeply discouraged. *(Combine the two sentences into one by adding an adjective.)*

During halftime, Coach Williams gave the discouraged players confidence in themselves.

1. Heather will not be at the party tomorrow. Brittany will not be there either. *(Combine the two sentences by writing one sentence with a compound subject.)*

   Neither Heather nor Brittany will be at the party tomorrow.

2. Todd held the tent up straight. Matthew hammered down the stakes. *(Combine the two sentences into one sentence by putting one idea into an adverb clause.)*

   While Todd held the tent up straight, Matthew hammered down the stakes.

3. Umar Shah lived in India before moving here. He is our new doctor. *(Combine the two sentences into a single sentence by using an appositive phrase. Place the phrase next to the noun it modifies. Put commas at the beginning and end of the appositive phrase.)*

   Umar Shah, our new doctor, lived in India before moving here.

4. In August, Lindsay visited her grandparents in Orlando. She also toured Universal Studios. *(Combine the two sentences into a single sentence with one subject and a compound verb.)*

   In August Lindsay both visited her grandparents in Orlando and toured Universal Studios.

5. Christina hurried off the stage. She was grinning from ear to ear. *(Combine the two sentences into one sentence by using a verb phrase.)*

   Grinning from ear to ear, Christina hurried off the stage.

BONUS:

Write several items with at least two or three short, choppy sentences. Then, edit each item into one sentence. Give an unedited version to a classmate to edit.

Proofreading for Clarity, Transition, and Order
Cumulative Review
Paragraphing, Word Order, Transitions, Wordiness, and Sentence Vari~~ety~~

ACTIVITY: The following report on Robert Frost contains no e~~rrors~~ ~~in~~ punctuation, or capitalization; however, it does contain error~~s~~ ~~in paragraphing,~~ word order, **transitions, wordiness,** and **sentence va**~~riety.~~

Edit the report using the sentence combining methods you have learned. Be careful not to change the meaning of the original report. Use the proofreading symbols to correct all errors. Then, rewrite the corrected report on a separate sheet of paper.

A TRADITIONAL POET, ROBERT FROST

Robert Frost was one of America's leading twentieth-century poets. He was a four-time winner of the Pulitzer Prize. *since* Frost grew up in New England. Many of his poems are about the countryside in winter. His poetry is traditional. It is also experimental and universal. Frost's importance as a poet evolved from the power of particular poems. One poem has been popular with students. The poem is entitled "Stopping by Woods on a Snowy Evening." In this poem a traveler pauses on a journey. The traveler pauses for a moment. The journey is by horse and wagon. The traveler watches the snow. The snow is falling in the woods. The woods are far from the nearest village. *Although* People disagree about the poem's meaning. They enjoy it immensely. It touches on a deep truth about life. Frost received an unusual number of literary honors. He also received a range of academic and public honors. Robert Frost unquestionably succeeded in realizing his life's ambition: to write "a few poems that will be hard to get rid of."

Proofreading and Editing Activities for Writing

The activities in this chapter will use all of the proofreading practices previously covered in this book. You will: (a) edit a letter to a pen pal, using correct spelling, capitalization, and punctuation; (b) proofread for errors in language usage in a thank-you letter and a business letter; (c) proofread for clarity, transition, and order in a book report; and (d) edit an outline, a report, and a bibliography using all of the skills of proofreading.

Working through these exercises will improve your proofreading confidence as well as your writing skills.

ACTIVITY: Proofread the following letter to a pen pal, using the proofreading symbols (see page 5) to correct the errors in **spelling, punctuation,** and **capitalization.** Then, copy the corrected letter on a separate sheet of paper.

4356 westwind Drive
Edmond, Ok 73013
Janary 5, 1997

Dear Conrad,

I had a wonderful christmas vacation with my family in Oklahoma city. We spent the Holidays with my Grandmother. Our family had so much fun caroling on christmas eve. How did you celebrate your holidays in Munich? I hope your vacation was as enjoyable as mine. School begins tomorrow. I am not looking forward to going back. I have been chosen as class reporter for our School Newspaper. I am woried that I will not have enough time for my schoolwork. Our newspaper is called *The Chatter Box.* Does your school have a newspaper?

You may be wondering why this letter is typed. My Mother has moved her office to our house. And she is letting me use her computer. are you impressed? I have learned so much in the last month about computers. Do you have a home-computer? I have inclosed a picture of our neighborhood. Please send me a picture of what Munich looks like in the Winter. I will write to you again as soon as I here from you.

your pen pal,

Josh

Proofreading and Editing Activities for Writing
Proofreading for Errors in Language Usage

ACTIVITY: Proofread the following thank-you note for errors in **language** ~~usage including~~ **subject-verb agreement, sentence fragments, run-o**~~ns, double~~ negatives, and misplaced modifiers. Correct the~~se using~~ ~~proofreading~~ symbols (see page 5). Then, copy the corre~~cted note on a se~~parate sheet of paper.

79 Chuckwagon Trail
Casper, WY 82604
September 5, 1996

Dear Kendall,

Since I returned home, *I have* been thinking about the marvelous week I spent with you and your family in Yellowstone National Park. The park had always been a picture album place to me, and now I have my own photos, but the outdoor scenery *was* only part of the enjoyment I experienced with your family.

Waking up in the morning to the smell of bacon and eggs, hiking up the steep trails, and sitting around the campfire singing songs, I will long remember all of these things. I will not never forget the morning we were awakened to the sound through our trash cans of the grizzly bear rummaging. What a way to wake up!

Please tell your mother as soon as they are developed I will send her some of the photos. Thanks again for such an enjoyable and relaxing week.

Your friend,

Alexa Rae

To the Teacher: You may choose to make a transparency of this activity for use on the overhead. Then, ask for class participation.

Panel 63

63

Proofreading and Editing Activities for Writing
Proofreading for Errors in Spelling, Capitalization, Punctuation, and Language Usage

ACTIVITY: Proofread the following book report on *The Witch of Blackbird P___* in spelling, capitalization, punctuation, subject-verb agree___ ___ ___nces, sentence fragments, and paragraphing. Use the ___ ___ ___ading symbols (see page 5) to correct the report.

Answers may vary

The Witch of Blackbird Pond
Thomas Ashley McCoy IV

The Witch of Blackbird Pond *was written* by Elizabeth George Speare, a famous author of other historical novels. This enjoyable, entertaining book, first published in 1958, is a newbery award winner.

The story take place during the Nineteenth century in Connecticut Colony. The main character is Katherine Tyler, also known as "Kit" this fictional book has many other interesting characters, especially Hannah, an old widow who becomes a close friend of Kit. Kit sails on a ship called the Dolphin to Wetherfield, a town in Connecticut, leaving the Caribbean Islands. With no one to turn to she hopes that her only living relatives will accept her. Kit finds herself in a strange and lonely place quite different from the sunny Caribbean Islands where she once lived. In the strict Puritan community home of her relatives, she works long, tiring hours. The only place she feels free and pieceful is at Blackbird Pond, where she can let go of her worries.

Panel 64

64

Proofreading and Editing Activities for Writing
Book Report, Continued

One day Kit wanders into a meadow and meets Hannah, the Witch of Black bird Pond. When their friendship is discovered kit is accused of whichcraft. Suddenly a mysterious fever spreads throughout the town. A few children die from this illness. Suspecting that she put an evil curse on the town. The angry people decide to burn Hannah's home.

I enjoyed this book. The characters thoughts and actions seemed especially believable. Kit, my favorite character in the book, reminds me of several of my outspoken friends. Ms. Speare wrote this historical novel with excitement and zest. I highly recommend The Witch of Blackbird Pond because it is quite heartwarming and enlightening.

SPECIAL NOTE: There are over 30 corrections needed in the book report. Did you find all the errors? If not, reread the book report to see if you can find the errors you missed.

Panel 65

65

Proofreading and Editing Activities for Writing
Proofreading for Errors in an Outline

ACTIVITY: Carefully proofread the following outline for errors in the use of **Roman numerals, Arabic numerals,** and **capital letters.** Use the proofreading symbols (see page 5) to correct the errors. Copy the corrected outline on a separate sheet of paper.

Beginning a Coin collection

I. Reasons for collecting coins
  a. Pleasure
    1. Fun of watching collection grow
    2. appreciating variety of coins
  b. Educational value
    1. Learning location of countries
    2. Learning about people and customs
II. Sources for the collector
  A. loose change
  B. local bank
  c. hobby stores
  D. coin dealers
    1. Catalogs
    2. Proof sets
iii. Display for coins
  a. Supplies
    1. Collection book
    2. Gloves
    3. plastic sleeves
  b. Procedure
    1. checking coin
    2. inserting coin
IV. Specialty for coins

SPECIAL NOTE: There are 25 corrections needed in the outline. Did you find all the errors? If not, reread the outline to see if you can find the errors you missed.

Panel 67

67

Proofreading and Editing Activities for Writing
Proofreading Longer Selections for Errors

ACTIVITY: Proofread the following report "The Amish: Who Are They?" by Jonath___ ___ ___y. Use the proofreading symbols (see page 5) to correct errors in spellin___ ___ ___n, capitalization, language usage, wordiness, transition, ___ ___ ___ corrected report on a separate sheet of paper.

The Amish: Who Are
by Jonathan McCoy

Answers may vary

The Amish have a different way of life than any other people around them. The Amish have always lived by their religious beliefs and followed the teachings of the Bible. The Amish aquired their name from Joseph Amman. Amman and his followers stressed a simple life. He stressed strict church discipline. They believed in kicking out excommunicated members.

The Amish group in the seventeenth century originated in Switzerland. William Penn invited them to the New World to settle in Pennsylvania. They welcomed the opportunity to escape religious persecution and go to a place in order to live in peace. From 1710 to the end of the eighteenth century, the Amish settled along the streams and fertile valleys in Southeastern Pennsylvania. At present the largest population of the Amish is located in Ohio. Throughout the United States there are approximately 92,000 Amish.

Last summer my family and I visited an Amish community in Lancaster County, Pennsylvania. We toured a village where the homes were not like the homes of most Americans. In an Amish home they do not have electricity. In an Amish home there are no radios, televisions, or any other modern appliances. Coal, gas, or oil powered heaters are their only sources of heat. The Amish also have gas-powered refrigerators. Kerosene lamps or lamps are their main sources of light that burn naphtha. The Amish don't have no running water other than a small water pump that is used in the kitchen. Other sources of water must be pumped from an outdoor pump and carried into the house.

Meals are prepared and eaten in the kitchen, the largest and most commonly used room in the house. The kitchen is also used for playing games, reading, sewing, and doing schoolwork. All rooms, especially the kitchen, are kept in spotless condition.

The Amish hold their worship services on Sunday. They are a very Christian group. Their services, sometimes held in members' homes or in a barn, begin at eight in the morning and last until noon. Men and Women are seated on wooden benches on different sides of the room. These worship services are usually attended by twenty-five to thirty families. The host family serves lunch to the congregation.

©1999 by Incentive Publications, Inc.
Nashville, TN.

Proofreading and Editing Activities for Writing

Proofreading Longer Selections for Errors, Continued

School is held in a one-room schoolhouse. The Amish children study spelling, penmanship, English, reading, and grammar. They also study arithmetic, social studies, and the Bible. Students attend school through the eighth grade from kindergarten. The Amish do not see a need for education beyond the eighth grade since they will be farming for a living. The school teacher is usually a young, unmarried Amish woman who has also only an eighth-grade education. She has been an apprentice in a classroom for two years. Amish children do not attend public schools because their parents do not want their children influenced by those not of their faith.

One way to identify an Amish person is by their dress. Most Amish clothing is homemade. Amish women are taught to sew at an early age. The women usually wear long, black, blue, or green dresses. Aprons are always worn over their dresses. If a woman is married the apron is black, however, if she is unmarried, the apron is white. White caps are also worn. Jewelry or colorful clothes are not allowed. Men dress in black or dark suits. Suspenders which do not have buttons or zippers are used to hold up their pants. Instead they have hook and eye fasteners. A black felt hat or straw hat completes their wardrobe. Like their parents the Amish boys and girls dress. Men that are married must have beards but not mustaches.

Ownership of a farm is the primary goal of an Amish family. The Amish work hard on their farms. They take pride in them. Their farms are neat but not very large. Amish farm equipment has steel wheels and is powered by horses, mules, or both. If neighbors need equipment, he will lend it to them. The Amish crops usually consist of corn, barley, wheat, and a variety of vegetables. Tobacco is sometimes raised as a cash crop.

Amish funerals are rather standard. Both men and women are buried in white. After a person dies, he or she is buried three days later unless that day is a Sunday. The coffin is constructed of wood. The coffin is taken to the cemetery in a horse-drawn hearse. Because no flowers are laid on the grave, the only marker is a tombstone. I found it interesting that the Amish believe in life after death, and their after-life is based on their earthly life.

Though my research, I have learned that the Amish people are deeply religious; they dress very simply; they do not use modern conveniences; and they are dedicated to farming. Although the outside world has been changing rapidly, the Amish only change and use new technology if it does not conflict with their basic beliefs.

SPECIAL NOTE: There are over 40 corrections needed in the report. Did you find all of the errors? If not, reread the report to see if you can find the errors you missed.

Proofreading and Editing Activities for Writing

Proofreading a Bibliography

ACTIVITY: Proofread the following bibliography (*a list of sources alphabetized by the last name of the author or the first word of the title*). Use the proofreading symbols (see page 5) to correct the errors in form, spelling, punctuation, and capitalization. Copy the corrected bibliography on a separate sheet of paper.

BIBLIOGRAPHY

Amish Country. Gettysburg, Pennsylvania: TEM, Inc, 1988.

Bender, Harold S., and Smith, Henry C. "Mennonites and Their Heritage." Mennonite Encyclopedia. Scottdale, Pennsylvania: Good Books, 1964.

Davies, Blodwen. String of Amber: The Heritage of the Mennonites. Scottdale, Pennsylvania: Herald Press, 1973.

Denlinger, A. Martha. real People. Scottdale, Pennsylvania: Herald Press, 1986.

Hostetler, John A. Amish life. Scottdale, Pennsylvania: Herald Press, 1983.

"Mennonites." Grolier Multimedia Encyclopedia. CD-ROM. 1993.

Redekop, C.W. Mennonite Society. Scottdale, pennsylvania: Good Books, 1989.

Dyck, Cornelius J., ed. Introduction to Mennonite History. Scottdale, Pennsylvania: Herald Press, 1981.

Scott, Stephen, and Pellman, Kenneth. Living Without Electricity. Scottdale, Pennsylvania: Good Books, 1990.

Williams, George H. The Radical Reformation. Gettysburg, Pennsylvania: Gettysburg Press, 1962.

SPECIAL NOTE: There are approximately 16 corrections needed in the bibliography. Did you find all of the errors? If not, reread the bibliography to see if you can find the errors you missed.

Building Proofreading Skills